the dangerous actor

Judith Gick actress, director, playwright, teacher of acting

Judith was born in 1908 – the same year that the first British drama school was established – and her teaching credentials are unique.

Her early acting experience was in the prestigious Benson Company, headed by Donald Wolfit, and this was followed by years of experience in repertory theatre and television.

Her drama school work began at RADA and continued for fifteen years under the principalships of John Fernald and Hugh Cruttwell. As well as directing productions and running individual acting tutorials, she was responsible for devising the Academy's Jubilee programme *Ever Since Aeschylus* – attended by the Queen and the Queen Mother.

In 1968 she lectured and taught at Lyola University, Chicago, directed *Three Sisters* and became deeply involved in the problems of student unrest, devising and directing a programme which looked at the role of the theatre at such a time.

For the twenty-three years before her retirement in 1995, she worked with Raphael Jago at Webber Douglas and started classes for the study of Shakespeare text. This developed into exercises based on the one-person show which soon became an integral feature of the school's training.

Superstars, household names and hundreds of other actors solidly respected in the profession have passed through her acting classes. She has left her individual mark on all of them.

Her playwriting credits include *The Common Story, The Golden Thread,* the first stage adaptation of Dylan Thomas' *Doctor and the Devils, Mistress Mine* and *The Singer's Tale.* The two latest titles are one-woman shows which have been performed in Britain and abroad by Anna Barry, Judith's daughter by Michael Barry, who was Head of Drama at BBC Television 1951-61 and Principal of LAMDA 1972-78.

Judith lives in North London and is currently working on a novel based on the relationship between Shakespeare and Anne Hathaway.

the
dangerous actor

a support book for actors in training

judith gick

Virtual Angels Press

the dangerous actor

First published in the United Kingdom in 1997 by
Virtual Angels Press
67c St Peter's Street London N1 8JR

A CIP catalogue record for this book is available
from the British Library

ISBN 0 9526303 1 1

Set in Caslon

Printed in the United Kingdom by Biddles Limited
Woodbridge Park, Guildford, Surrey GU1 1DA

for you

contents

TECHNIQUE

Blueprint: A less interesting character?

PRACTICALITIES

Blueprint: Finding the part

BOOKS

Blueprint: Interesting problems

ENDING

preface

When I first began to teach at RADA many years ago, I was somewhat daunted by the students. My only previous experience had been directing professionals. Suddenly, here I was confronted with a group of people who did not know much at all about acting, to whom theatrical terms were a strange language. Fortunately many of my colleagues were not only gifted artists and splendid teachers, but wonderfully helpful to new people like myself.

There was a small hell-hole under the stairs which was known as the staff cloakroom (ladies) where much serious discussion took place on what to do with students and how to do it. After work, some of us would go across to the ristorante in Goodge Street to continue our talk over a plate of spaghetti. There was one staff member with whom I frequently sat talking about acting. She was a splendid actress and a splendid, though terrifying, teacher. The presence of students weeping on the stairs was a sure sign that her class was just over. Minutes later, one would find her at lunch in the staff canteen. She would look up, beam and say warmly, 'They are very talented!'

She always had a five pound note tucked in a back pocket of her handbag. If a student was obviously struggling against odds, she would finish a severe criticism of his work with the sharp question, 'Are you getting enough to eat?' – as ever, student grants were swallowed up in high rents and fares. While the student was struggling to reply, the fiver would be produced and handed over with the instruction to get a good meal and act better tomorrow. Then she would come to the hell-hole and say to any of us who happened to be there, 'The boy's brilliant but they do need a steak sometimes.'

For me, there was a never-to-be-forgotten occasion in the ristorante one evening – I think we had pushed the boat out and we were having a glass of wine with our meal – when she said, 'You know, my dear, you learn from your students.'

She did not mean the student who has studied the play at university and quotes what his tutor had to say, or the one who has played Juliet in the school play, but the one who wants to know, the student to whom she had to say, 'I don't know, I'll look it up', who makes learning a shared experience and one that never ends. As I continued in my teaching this is what I discovered too: the richness, the exploration, the discovery that can occur so unexpectedly, so quietly, so strangely; the magic that happens between artist and pupil.

Judith Gick
London 1996

*a*cknowledgments

This book is based on what I have learnt from working at RADA with John Fernald and, after him, with Hugh Cruttwell; with Yat Malgrem; the work I did in partnership with that great teacher of singing, Florence Norberg; and finally, with Raphael Jago at the Webber Douglas Academy of Dramatic Art. His good nature, patience, insight and courage allowed me to make many experiments in the teaching of acting. His support was always there.

The book came about because of those students who wanted 'all that written down', who read it as I wrote and told me what they wanted. I am grateful to them and to my colleagues on the staff who gave me help and encouragement.

Some of the many quotations in this book required the permission of various authors and publishers. I should like to acknowledge the following for kindly permitting me to quote from their published authors:

Faber and Faber for *No Man's Land* by Harold Pinter, Penguin Books for their edition of *Beowulf* translated by Michael Alexander, Methuen for *Gotcha* by Barrie Keeffe, and the Society of Authors on behalf of the Bernard Shaw Estate for *Heartbreak House* by George Bernard Shaw.

foreword by Robert Lind**s***a***y**

Ms Gick was my private tutor in the second half of my period at RADA between 1968 and 1970.

She was and is a woman of great beauty and crystal-clear intellect, but the most important thing of value she passed on to me was her understanding of language and its use.

I noticed in reading her book that she comments on how actors sometimes, rather foolishly, improvise some of the text in an attempt to memorise some of their lines. This can be a big mistake, especially if the text has the stature of a Shaw, Ibsen or Shakespeare.

As an actor, one has to trust the text completely – although in this day and age as we enter into the abyss of mediocrity as far as television writing is concerned, it is sometimes very difficult to trust what one has to say. This book will give back the confidence – to those who are willing to learn – that there are still great writers and great words to be spoken. Judith Gick will explain all.

Thy danger chiefly lies in acting well;
No crime's so great as daring to excel.

Charles Churchill (1731-1764) to William Hogarth

introduction: *a* kind of guide book

Some years ago, when I first thought of writing this book, a student said to me, 'Judith, you can never write a book. Your classes are you. We like them because we never know what is going to happen.' What he did not realise was that it was he and other students who caused the variations to happen. One can plan a lesson, make notes, bring them into class, then a student does something lovely, strange, original, even bad, but it has to be talked about, seen in relation not only to what the student has done, but to what is wonderful in theatre.

One cannot isolate completely the problems of acting. In painting it is possible to teach students how to put on a wash, to give them the rules of perspective and the theory of colour, without referring to the needs of the student in the picture he is endeavouring to paint. But the actor is his own instrument: it is not possible to make so clear a distinction between the different 'subjects'.

Classes in voice, movement, improvisation and text are taken separately, so that the actor can, as far as possible, isolate problems and so that he can think and practise only one aspect of his art. But the actor's physicality affects his voice, and his vocal flexibility affects his ability to deal with text. So, because you cannot separate the functions of the actor you will find a certain amount of repetition; and if this book is a bit haphazard it is because I write as far as possible as if I were talking to students, answering questions that I remember having been asked.

It may seem odd that I have taken nearly all the text examples from Shakespeare. Some students are apprehensive about approaching Shakespeare. Some may have been at a school where it was badly taught. Some may never have read any at all. Some have told me that they did not know Shakespeare wrote about real people. Others have thought you ought to have a special way of acting Shakespeare. One told me he had believed that you had to shout and wave your arms about! Furthermore, the opportunities for working in a Shakespearian company, or even in one of the great national companies, are nothing like as frequent as working in modern plays, films and TV. But – and it is a very big but – the old actors used to say that if you could play Shakespeare you could play anything. They were right. Shakespeare makes the biggest demands emotionally, physically and intellectually, but the rewards are the greatest.

There is another very practical reason for studying Shakespeare. If I had chosen examples from many different periods you would be put to great expense buying the playtexts, or have to depend on their availability at the library. But Shakespeare texts are widely available and they are cheap. Drama students are often asked to bring the complete works of Shakespeare when they begin a course. Nearly every tutor will at some time refer to Shakespeare and quite often ask you to learn a few lines in order to show how some particular aspect of voice or movement is necessary in acting.

Shakespeare never lets you down. He was an actor writing for actors. He does not seem to have thought of himself as someone special. If you want to know how he felt his plays should be acted, you have it all in the advice to the Players in Act III of *Hamlet* which is quoted in full at the beginning of SPEECH, the second part of this book.

If you are thinking of going to drama school, or if you have just finished and are going to audition for professional work, I suggest you read over very carefully Hamlet's advice to the Players. You may find you have to go very carefully over these lines:

> to hold, as 'twere, the mirror up to nature; to show virtue her own feature, scorn her own image, and the very age and body of the time his form and pressure.

He is asking his actors to present honestly (with love as well as hatred – but always with understanding) the human beings portrayed in his plays, and to show how those human beings are affected by the social and political pressures of the time in which they live.

I find that most young people, no matter from what background, are basically compassionate. It is they who are the first to say, 'It is not fair.' I remember it in myself when I was no more than eleven. How could I become an actress and yet make the world a better place in which to live? That can be the artist's dilemma. As Hamlet says, 'The time is out of joint. O cursed spite that ever I was born to set it right.'

When I set out to organise the notes I had accumulated for this book, I found I did not know where to begin. Then a friend who has himself taught at various drama schools said, 'That is the question all first term students ask. Where to begin?' They mean of course, 'How do I begin work on the part I have been given?'

The first few weeks, maybe the first term, at drama school is a period of discovery and adjustment. The staff are strangers and one's fellow students are strangers. One is bombarded with information: the rules of the school and its geography. The main subjects in the timetable – acting, voice and movement, singing and musical training. There seems to be very little time between classes, and that is frequently taken up moving from one venue to another, or changing for movement, or back after movement. For many students London is a strange city, in some cases a foreign one. Where to live and where to eat, which train or bus to catch, are all problems that have to be coped with. No wonder students feel that some of the teaching gets a bit lost in this early period.

When I talked with some of them about the idea of this book, they were quite definite that they wanted something simple. Not 'Six Easy Lessons in Acting' but a kind of guide book. Something that would help beginners through those difficult first weeks. A book that could be used on those occasions when something had been said in class that had not been understood and shyness prevented a question. Not because you were afraid of the tutor, but because you were scared of your fellow students, some of whom seemed much more knowledgeable and sophisticated than you. Then there were times when a class was missed through illness and a vital piece of information had gone astray.

Before starting, I read or re-read as many of the books on acting as I could find from Stanislavski on — and I understood the student's plea for something simple. There are some fine books about acting, but they all seem to me to presume a basic knowledge. Several actors have said to me that they only really understood Stanislavski's *An Actor Prepares* after they had been in the theatre for some time. Frankly, his book is not a big help in your first acting project at drama school because there is too much of it.

The important thing to grasp is that all present-day acting is Stanislavski-based. His teaching has become part of the texture of theatrical life. He himself learnt from watching and talking with the great actors and directors of his day. He collected and collated everything he could about acting.

Many other actors and directors have written fascinatingly about their own approach to acting, but like Stanislavski they all seem to be talking or writing for people who already know something about it.

So, to begin at the beginning … what is acting?

acting

The stage is always beginning
anew; the candidates for
theatrical reputation are
always setting out afresh,
unencumbered   by   the
affectation of the faults of
others or by the excellence of
their predecessors.

William Hazlitt
On Actors and Acting
1817

1 What is acting?

In spite of all the impressions the new student is getting, and perhaps the slight bewilderment he is feeling, overriding everything is the need to do well in his first role.

This is as it should be. An actor's instinct makes it his first priority. He is here because he loves acting and wants to do it as well as he can, not just in the hope of getting good notes from the staff at the end of term, but for his own artistic satisfaction. He knows that in the professional theatre he would be concentrating on rehearsal to the exclusion of all else, so it seems strange that in the first terms at drama school so few hours are devoted to acting. It is difficult to see how all the classes – voice, speech, movement and singing – are to be of immediate help to him. Of course, the reasons for it all are explained by the principal and the various tutors concerned: much of the preliminary work of the technical classes consists of explaining to students the reason for what they are doing and the ultimate object of it all. Time must be taken to explore the individual needs, potential and personality of each student. The student will find himself in a rehearsal situation before he has had anything much in the way of practical know-how. Technical training is a long process and cannot be hurried. While most students accept this, they do not at first realise that technical classes can be creative, and that mastering all these different skills will give them the one thing they are greedy for – excellence in acting.

Never before have actors had such demands made on them. If an actor is to become first rate, that is to say, if he has the ability to work to the highest level in every branch of his chosen art, he must be expert in every style from the classical theatre of ancient Greece to tap-dancing in a modern musical. So, at drama school students are introduced gradually to the rehearsal procedure and the acting experience: a few hours of rehearsal a week, culminating in the demonstration of what has been achieved to the principal and those members of the technical staff who have been working with them.

Too much acting, too soon, can mean not the elimination but the ironing in of faults. If the student does not fully understand this process there may be restlessness and frustration in the first weeks of the course. It is particularly difficult for students who have previously done a lot of amateur work. In its own sphere much amateur work is excellent but there is frequently a basic difference of approach between the student's previous experience and what is now being asked of him. An intelligent student will assess this difference and work out what he must discard and what can be of use to him in his new environment.

The most important thing a student must realise is that **drama schools do not teach acting**. Drama schools provide a great many skills that the student needs in order to act well but **you teach yourself to act**. So the first question to be asked must be, 'What is acting?' When I have asked beginner students that question in their first class there has usually been a long silence. They all know that they very much want to act, but they have never really asked themselves what acting is. I am sure I did not at their age.

In answer to that question, someone might suggest that acting is the creation of a character. True, but characters are created in other art forms. A novelist creates his by writing about them. Think of characters created by Dickens, Cervantes and by Charlotte and Emily Brontë. And what about a painter? He, too, creates characters. Go to the gift shop of any great art gallery and you will find postcard reproductions of pictures. Many are of a single person: the child watching the Annunciation in Crevelli's great *Annunciation*; Franz Hals' portrait of *The Laughing Cavalier* – so popular that it once adorned nearly every biscuit box or tea-caddy. That enigmatic creation of Leonardo da Vinci, the *Mona Lisa*, is similarly ubiquitous today. It is clear that the creation of character is not limited to the actor. In what way, then, does the art of an actor differ? What is acting?

The answer is in the word 'acting'. Look it up in a dictionary and this is the kind of definition you will find:

> **act**, *v.i.* to present, to perform a play or part, to personate (character or play in life), to perform actions...from the Latin *agere*, to do.

It is the final definition which is important to us at this moment. **Acting is doing**. It is by showing the actions of a character from moment to moment that the actor reveals a whole personality. The audience only knows what it sees and what it hears, so the actor must use his physical equipment, his body and his voice, to give the relevant information – to tell the audience what he wants them to know.

But what he wants them to know is created in his own psyche, in his own personality. The actor is his own person. His instrument is not just his body and his voice. The all-important qualities – his creative imagination, his observation and his experience of life – are not visible. These qualities are his and his alone. No-one but he can understand what is happening to him, what messages these qualities give to his creative self. At a good drama school he should find that these qualities are being developed and guided; but even in the acting classes, in which he will discover much about acting, he will come to realise that he alone can provide the real creativity. He is responsible for himself. He must respect his talent and cultivate it. It is up to him to use his drama school.

This is why one cannot teach acting. It is because these qualities belong to the artist and cannot be understood by anyone else unless he chooses to communicate what he thinks and feels. He uses these three qualities – imagination, observation, experience – to examine the character he is called upon to play. He then works to express through physical action what he feels. 'Acting is physical' is what I was told as a young actress, and it is true. Everything you do on the stage is a gesture, even the flick of an eyelid. Do not do anything unless you mean to do it.

We will be looking in detail at PHYSICALITY and GESTURE in couple of later sections. But first I want to consider these three qualities and their importance for the artist.

2 Imagination, observation and experience

Imagination is the artist's first and finest quality. Without it he does not exist. Imagination is the core of his personality. But we must define what it is. And also what it is not. Imagination is not dreaming or fantasising. If you want to understand the distinction very clearly, read the famous short story by James Thurber, *The Secret Life of Walter Mitty*.

The actor-artist has to consider what Keats meant when the poet spoke of 'the truth of imagination'. He surely meant the ability to think oneself into the mind and feelings of another human being as deeply as it is possible for one soul to understand another.

Observation is the second quality which the actor uses to feed his imagination. He must be aware of how people behave and how they think and react to ideas. He needs to know more than just their physical mannerisms. A performer who works on these alone is not an actor, he is a mimic – though the actor will at times make use of mimicry in his acting. When he watches people he is not only noting what they do, but asking himself why they do it. What are the inner qualities that the physical and vocal mannerisms express?

The third quality is experience, or more exactly, **related experience**. In his books, Stanislavski refers to this quality as 'emotion memory'. This is a term which I have ceased to use because the word 'emotion' conjures up for most of us a dramatic and uncontrolled display of feeling. The young actor feels he must shed tears, become passionate, even violent. The result of the misunderstanding causes him to become not more truthful but less.

What is meant by related experience? Well, the actor searches his memory for something that he has experienced that is in some way related to what is happening to the character. He does not play his own feeling but uses it to empathise with the character. It does not matter how slight the experience. It is a guide, a yardstick, by which the actor can measure the truth of what he is doing.

Recently, I was working with an actress on Beatrice from *Much Ado About Nothing*. She was having problems in understanding Beatrice's behaviour with Benedick. She found it hard to find any related experience. There was a long pause, then she suddenly burst out, 'I remember. There was a boy at school I was mad about, but I didn't want him or anyone else to know. I went on just like Beatrice, being as rude as I knew how – but secretly wanting him to like me.' There was another pause and then came the pay-off, 'I'm glad he didn't like me. He was horrid.' She then got to her feet and started to rehearse Beatrice very well.

You see, it does not always have to be a deeply serious experience, though indeed it may be. In the latter case one must be careful. If the experience you are called upon to play corresponds to a traumatic experience in your own life, the death of someone dear to you, something which is still deeply painful or something that is of very recent occurrence, then it is possible that you will find yourself unable to tackle it, or you will find yourself going out of control. It is best to discuss this in private with your director, or with a member of staff whom you find sympathetic. They will help you to see how the situation differs from your own, that the character, not being you, is dealing with the situation differently.

You discover your character by the use of imagination, observation and related experience. Your observation of people will suggest to you their physical being. Your imagination will suggest what might be going on in their mind, what they are feeling. The search for your own related experience will open up ways of giving expression to the character. This interaction of body and mind is all-important.

But how, practically, to use these qualities in preparing a part? What I shall do next – and at intervals throughout the book – is to look in detail at the approach to a specific part. I call this preparation 'making a blueprint'. You will find a blueprint after each of the main sections of the book.

3 Preparing a part: Orlando

Our first look at preparing a part is a breakdown of a short scene involving Orlando from Shakespeare's *As You Like It*. I have chosen this character as he is not very popular with actors. I have never heard one say he wants to play him.

If I were to choose a much loved part you might find that you were stuck with my blueprint when cast for the part sometime later in your career. If that should happen, what you find here should not impede you, but you will wish, I hope, to make your own analysis using this example as a guide.

For girl students the choice is more difficult because there are fewer women's parts and it was almost impossible to find one on which you would not be work-ing at some time in the near future, so I have chosen the characters of Rosalind and Celia from *As You Like It*. You will find the blueprint for this in the next sec-tion. But first let us consider Orlando.

Work on the project will, of course, begin by reading and discussing the play. Then the director will decide on the material he is going to use and decide on the casting. This will not happen immediately because he will need some time to get to know his actors and their potential.

We will presume that you have been given Orlando's second scene (Act I Scene ii). I have chosen this one because here he first comes into contact with several other people and important things happen to him.

In the reading of the play and the discussion you will have formed some ideas about the character of Orlando. Now make a great imaginative leap. Do what you did when you were a child playing a pretend game. You said to yourself, 'I am Robin Hood, or Charlie Chaplin, or Superman' or whoever it was that you want-ed to be – and you believed it. You went ahead and did what the character did. Of course, there was a strong element of fantasy about it, and although you sometimes invented most of the dialogue and added new elements to the story, you stuck firmly to what you believed to be true of the character. Any children playing with you who made alterations which you felt were wrong were well and truly bashed.

Here are two questions you are going to have to ask yourself and keep on asking yourself now and always, whatever part you are playing: What am I doing? Why am I doing it?

First of all, list the actions. What do I do? Do this very simply even if it does seem a bit daft. Try as much as you can to think of the character in the first person. You are trying to identify with him so start by thinking of him as yourself.

1. I enter with the Duke, lords and attendants.

2. I answer Le Beau and tell him I will attend the princesses.

3. I answer Rosalind and tell her that I have not challenged Charles, the wrestler, but like the others have accepted his challenge.

4. After both girls have asked me not to go on with the wrestling match I let them know that I am determined to go through with it. Then I say it does not really matter if I am killed because I do not amount to much.

5. I then respond to Charles who has rather rudely wanted to know why we are not getting on with it. I have two short speeches to him. In both I suggest he should not boast about about putting me down before doing it.

That is what I am doing as Orlando. Now let us go back over these questions, asking, 'Why am I doing it?'

1. I enter with the Duke, lords and attendants. They have for some reason chosen a different venue for this match. There are ten speeches before I say a word. Do I hear what is being said? Well, it would seem that I hear the Duke's first speech as he is speaking to all the people around him, but the the next few speeches surely I do not hear. These people are speaking about me. Of course, as actors and actresses they must speak loud enough to be heard by the audience, but I must appear not to hear them. So what am I doing? I am probably thinking about the way Charles fights. I have just seen him nearly kill three young men. Were they so hopelessly inexperienced that they should never have tried to fight him? Or has what I have seen told me that Charles is not all that skilled; that he relies on a few well-known tricks and his great weight to pull him through? In Scene i, I have complained furiously about my inadequate education, but one of the skills I might have learned among my brother's servants is how to wrestle well. I may be thinking of these things while pulling off my sweater, or in some way preparing for the fight.

2. So Le Beau speaking to me as he does disturbs my concentration, and what he says is somewhat of a surprise inasmuch as I am not used to being sum-

moned into the presence of royal ladies. However, from my reply it would seem that my formal education has not been all that bad. My next line is a reply to Rosalind. So it would seem after having replied to Le Beau, I immediately cross to the princesses. Do I bow? Do I know in what period the director is setting the play? Bows differ from period to period. Anyway, Orlando may not have been instructed in how to bow in the presence of royalty. So play safe, stand erect and make a very slight but dignified bow – the sort of thing I have seen people do when presented to royalty.

3. I reply very politely to the princess who has spoken to me and explain that it is Charles who has issued a challenge to anyone who dare fight him. I am just one of several who have accepted it. Why? I have been asked a question and answer it correctly.

4. I have a speech of several lines in which I explain why I must go on with the fight. Why? It is not mentioned, but it would seem to be understood in this society, and in spite of persuasion, I would be thought a coward if I did not fight. Anyway, what would I think of myself? However, I do thank them for their kindness and consideration. That is the first half of the speech. The next half is a bit difficult because I might seem self-pitying. So perhaps I assure them that it is alright, it does not matter, I am not that important. It is the kind of thing one says when one feels one is being worried about by very nice people.

5. I respond to Charles somewhat jauntily. Why? Have I been cheered by my contact with the princesses?

Now let us go over the whole thing again, this time not just considering what I do, but what everyone else does and how it concerns me.

1. When I enter with the Duke I know who I am and what has just happened to me from a careful study of the first scene. I know that I have had a row with my brother. It has come to physical violence. He has struck me and I have laid hands on him, in fact I have nearly choked him. Therefore, I must be fairly strong. What I, Orlando, do not know, and this is important, is that my brother has had an interview with Charles and has given him such a poor opinion of my character that Charles has agreed that it might be better if I did not survive the match. What I do know is that should I succeed, I could expect a fairly substantial reward and perhaps some paid position at the Duke's court, helping to train the youngsters in wrestling and some other sports. It would seem that I have made an intelligent decision in accepting Charles' challenge. Because of my lack of education and influence I stand little chance of getting a position at court or in a sphere of elegance, but since all the young noblemen have to be instructed in what are

known as the manly exercises – riding, fencing, wrestling and so forth – I might stand a chance of a good position in the 'sports department'. Might even succeed Charles as court wrestler. Of course, this fight is dangerous but my relationship with my brother means I must do something. All this is what I know about myself. It is not what I am going to try to act, but it will condition my behaviour. It is why I am here.

2. There are several lines before I speak. The Duke has the first speech to the effect that I am stubborn and persist in fighting Charles. He seems angry about it. The three previous matches have been violent but unexciting. The Duke uses the word 'entreated' which suggests he might have offered me some kind of financial inducement to stand down, which I have refused. Why? It seems I have some confidence in my own proficiency. I may not have the weight, but I may know a trick or two better than Charles. When I do throw Charles, and the Duke tries to stop the match, I say, 'I am not yet well breath'd.' So it would seem I have reason for persisting. Of course, that I win the match is something that I, the actor, know, but that I, Orlando, only feel fairly confident about. Do I notice the princesses? They must be some distance from me and with what I have on my mind I may just have noticed that there are a couple of women in the audience, but I would hardly have bothered to look at them. It is only when I hear what Le Beau has to say that I probably look past him and see that they are something special. I may pull down my sweater or jerkin and make an appropriate reply to Le Beau.

3. I go across to the two girls and make my bow. The taller of the two puts the question have I challenged Charles? I remember my manners and explain the situation, calling her 'fair princess' as would be proper even if she were ugly.

4. The other girl speaks to me. She seems really concerned. The first girl joins in and promises that my reputation will not suffer; they will make it all right with the Duke.

5. I thank them for their consideration in quite a courtly way. For someone with little education I am not doing badly. Then in the second half of the speech (more difficult) perhaps I am a bit overcome. They are very glamorous and I am not used to having anyone express concern for me. Yes, I should assure them that it is all right.

6. So when Charles shouts, I probably shout back, feeling enormously encouraged and confident. Actually, I reply pretty firmly to Charles in his own vernacular, turning the edge of the double meaning in his line.

Now go back over this and think what you have done. In each section there is something that concerns me. Everything that happens is action. I am either speaking or I am **listening**.

If I am listening, I am reacting and being changed by what someone else is saying; I am making up my mind about how to respond to what is being said. If I were not to listen carefully and be moved by what the girls say to me I could not reply as I do.

Every director and tutor will emphasise the importance of listening. The important thing to remember is that you must listen **as the character**. This is an important discovery. I must hear everything that is being said **as though it were being said for the first time**.

Having assembled quite a lot of information about your character mentally, now go over the information and consider him physically.

Well, I am physically strong, used to a lot of tough physical exercise. But judging by all that is said, it would seem that I win that wrestling match not through strength but skill. It would seem that I have trained my body well. It responds to my mind. I have good coordination. That means I carry myself well, in an easy relaxed way. Later in the play it appears that I have a sword and can use it. All young men in Shakespeare's time were trained to use a sword. Fencing promotes good coordination. So I, the actor, must try to think what has already been said to me in class about the correct use of my body. What if I have already been made aware of faults in this area? If I have to think of standing straight and not letting my head drop forward, how can I think as Orlando?

But if I do not try to stand and move as Orlando I am actually telling a lie about him. I am asking the audience to believe in a physicality that is not his. I must begin to try to feel physically as Orlando. I must imagine what it would be like to inhabit his body.

Where to begin?

You will have been given some basic instruction in good walking. As you get used to the exercises you begin to realise that it is easier and much pleasanter to use your body well than to use it badly. It becomes more flexible; there are more things you can do with speed and ease. Gradually you do them without having to think about them. All good technique eventually becomes instinct. But you are nowhere near that yet. In the meantime, start your work on Orlando by working on him physically

Observe the simplicity, ease and self-possession of some actors. Watch Clint Eastwood walk down a street. He should have played Coriolanus! Watch some of those old cowboy heroes. See how they move. Easily, without affectation. Some of them use a rolling walk but when they do so it is to create a visual effect.

Even before he speaks the audience know something about a character by the way he walks. Try to imagine yourself physically as Orlando. Practise it. Then speak your first line. Does the dignity you have found in your body make the line come out right? A cowboy does not speak like Orlando. He does not use the same words. But notice how Gary Cooper, or John Wayne, or any of the old great cowboy heroes sounded when they wanted to show respect. The words are different and the timbre of voice is not like mine, but the feeling – and consequently the use of voice – is the same.

4 Preparing a part: Rosalind

You are already beginning to realise that the voice comes right if the physicality is right. But before we go on to consider the subject of PHYSICALITY, we should first look at Act I Scene ii of *As You Like It* worked in the same way that it has been for Orlando. It is this scene in which Rosalind, too, first makes her appearance in the play.

1. The first speech is a response to Celia's request that I should be more cheerful. I tell her that I cannot forget my father who is banished.

2. I respond to Celia's declared affection for me.

3. Completely won over by her generosity, I promise to be more cheerful and suggest some amusing pastime. I ask her what she thinks of falling in love.

4. Celia seems to have a poor opinion of love so I ask what she would suggest.

5. She suggests making fun of the goddess Fortune in the hope of making her distribute her gifts more fairly.

6. I wish it were possible to do so because at present she not only distributes her gifts unfairly, but she is most unfair to women.

7. When Celia points out that she seems to make the pretty ones bad and the good ones plain, I respond by telling her that our looks are the business of Nature not Fortune.

8. Celia points out that a girl may be pretty, but an accident (of Fortune) can destroy her appearance. She goes on gaily to indicate that Touchstone, the Fool, who has arrived, has been sent by Fortune to put an end to the witty game.

9. I try to continue the game by pointing out that here Fortune has got the better of Nature.

10. Celia manages one last twist to the argument, then breaks off to call Touchstone, who tells her that her father wants her. Celia, surprised, asks if he was made the messenger. (It would be very unusual for the Duke to send

a jester on an errand to his daughter; not at all correct. He would send a gentleman-in-waiting. However, in this case, he may have sent Touchstone, perhaps because he knows there is a very friendly relationship between his daughter and his jester.) Touchstone swears by his honour that although he was not made the messenger, he was told to come for her. I am so surprised by this that I demand to know where he, a fool, learned to use such an oath.

11. Touchstone does what is expected of him. He gives a ludicrous explanation.

12. I back up Celia's demand for proof.

13. Touchstone is sharply reproved by Celia for speaking disrespectfully of her father. The mood of the scene changes but is interrupted by the arrival of Le Beau.

14. My comment on him suggests that he is the court gossip.

15. We are joking again now. I respond to Celia's mischievous remark about Le Beau with a quip of my own. All three of us now set about teasing Le Beau, using puns as a way of scoring off him. He tries to tell them about the wrestling match he has just watched but we, knowing the elaborate way he has of telling anything, keep interrupting with sharp comments. When he finally tells his story it is a disturbing one. The atmosphere changes. There is a pause before I say, 'Alas!'

16. After Celia and Touchstone have spoken seriously I ask if there is anyone else who cares to watch such a brutal sport? I then ask if we should stay to watch it.

17. Celia having said that we shall, I watch the Duke and his entourage as they come in, and I see Orlando and ask if he is the man who will fight Charles.

18. The Duke suggests that the ladies try to dissuade Orlando from fighting as he is no match for Charles. Summoned by Le Beau, Orlando comes to us. I ask him immediately if he has challenged Charles.

19. Orlando explains that he has accepted Charles' challenge which was a general one. Celia expresses her concern and tries to persuade Orlando to withdraw. I join in and tell him that no one will think the worse of him, and Celia and I will persuade the Duke to cancel the fight. Orlando insists that he must fight.

20. Celia and I both wish him well. The fight begins. I call out another wish. Then after watching for a moment or two I realise that he is doing well and

call out my delight. Charles is thrown and Orlando an easy victor. Then the Duke becomes unpleasant to the point of being insulting when he discovers that he is the youngest son of Sir Rowland de Boys. The Duke's behaviour disturbs Celia. I exclaim that Sir Rowland was my father's great friend and add that, had I known, I would have been even firmer in trying to prevent Orlando from wrestling with Charles.

21. I go with Celia to speak to Orlando. She is charming to him, but I take a chain that I have been wearing and I give it to him, explaining that, were I in a position to do so, I would have given him a larger reward. Then I suddenly suggest to Celia that we should go.

22. On the point of leaving, I stop and say Orlando has called us back. I say that I am not in a position to be proud. I return to Orlando and ask him if he called. There is no reply. Then, quite recklessly, I tell him that he has 'overthrown more than his enemies'.

23. Celia calls. I hastily bid Orlando farewell and go out with her.

Now I go over this material for the second time, asking the reason for everything I do.

At the start of the scene I am somewhat depressed. My first speech explains why. Am I frequently unhappy about my father? From what Celia says in Scene iii −

> I did not then entreat to have her stay;
> It was your pleasure, and your own remorse;
> I was too young that time to value her,
> But now I know her.   I iii 65-68

It would seem that both girls were very young when Duke Frederick usurped the country. So I am probably sad because I am finding it difficult to remember my father. I am living at the court as a poor relation, but the situation is made pleasant by Celia's affection. I respond to her mild reproach and real generosity by trying to suggest a game. Why do I make the suggestion about falling in love? Well, both girls are young, but this was a time when there was no future for girls except in marriage. Marriages were arranged but young people, especially women, hoped for love. Celia will probably be pushed into a political alliance, but Rosalind has no fortune. Most men wanted a dowry. Will she be sufficiently alluring for the dowry not to matter? Dare she allow herself to fall in love? Surely some such thoughts must be going through her mind. Celia, shrewd and practical, sees the reality of the situation. It is a battle of wits. Remember, like a game of tennis, the object of a game is to win. Launch the arguments with the same enjoyment and vigour. You really want to serve an ace!

(10) The game is interrupted by the arrival of Touchstone, who involves us in another game. I must watch carefully the relationship between him and Celia because it is I who suggest that we should take him with us to the Forest of Arden.

(13) Celia sees Le Beau coming. We enjoy joking about his determination to impart news. It would appear that what he has to say is usually trivial, and we make fun of what he is trying to say until we realise that he is speaking of a wrestling match in which three young men have been seriously hurt. I am appalled. Then I ask, should we watch this wrestling? Why do I do that? Is it perhaps a wish to see what can attract people in such a display?

(17) Celia having agreed to stay, we watch the arrival of the Duke and his attendants, and Charles and Orlando. When I see Orlando I am interested enough to ask if he is the man to fight Charles.

(18) When summoned by Le Beau, Orlando comes before us. I am sufficiently excited to forget that Celia should really speak first and ask, as though I can hardly believe it, if he has challenged Charles. Celia tries to persuade him to desist and I go on even further with the persuasion. Orlando is firm in his determination to go through with it. How do I feel about his statement that there is no one to care about him and that he has no real place in the world?

(20) I wish that I could help him. When the fight begins, it appears that both Celia and I are caught up in the excitement. After it is over, I am at once delighted to realise who Orlando is and aware that, had I known earlier, I would have entreated him even more strongly not to fight. Celia is shocked by her father's behaviour and suggests that we should go to Orlando to thank him and encourage him.

(21) I am becoming more and more attracted to this young man and, realising that he has had no reward, I do what I can by giving him my chain. I wait for him to speak. He says nothing, but continues to gaze at me so intently that I retreat to Celia.

(22) I hate to leave him. I pretend that he has called. I make use of my inferior position at court to say that it does not matter if I behave as I should not. I go back and ask Orlando if he has called. There is still no reply from him. Encouraged by his obvious admiration, I tell him he has 'overthrown more than his enemies'. Then, unable to get any further response, I leave with Celia.

5 Physicality

Acting is a physical process. That is to say, thoughts and feelings have to be expressed through the body. It is difficult at first to relate the inner creative process to the external presentation. But since all the audience ever knows is what it sees and what it hears, a visible and audible identity must be created.

Having gone through Orlando and Rosalind's first short scene from *As You Like It*, we deduced from the situations and the characters' reactions to them what they are thinking and feeling. We have even thought briefly about the physical presentation. We must now consider in more detail how to externalise what has been discovered. Even before learning the lines it is important to begin to inhabit the body of the character. Let us deal with Orlando first.

One must think about the qualities that condition him and make up his attitude to life in terms of his physique. The most obvious character whose whole attitude to life has been governed by his physique is, of course, Richard III. He tells us about it in two great soliloquies, one at the end of *Henry IV, Part Three* and the other at the opening of *Richard III*. This does not exempt the actor from imagining what life would be like to be so handicapped. It is when an actor does consider what effect such a disability might have had on himself as a personality that we get an interesting performance of Richard. If not, all that happens is a boring reproduction of Olivier in the film, or whichever actor has recently made a success in the part.

Richard is an extreme case. It is, oddly enough, more difficult for a young actor to find the physicality of a character who would probably be described as perfectly normal. What do we mean by that? That we have never noticed anything remarkable about him. So how is the student going to tackle the part of Orlando – the kind of young man who used to be thought of in theatrical terms as a straight juvenile and nowadays may be thought of as boring? Is he just there to give the actress playing Rosalind the opportunity to show what she can do? In the past, actors tended to be dismissive of such characters and not pleased when asked to play them. Now, in good productions, the actor is expected to consider such a character and his relationships much more deeply.

Start by considering his physical presence. He gets the better of his brother, wins the wrestling match in record time and makes a powerfully romantic impression on Rosalind. How is a student actor to make all this convincing? It would seem that the actor cast for Orlando should be a hefty chap and glamorous. Like the actors one sees bouncing around in those old 1930s films. Well, they were there because they looked right. With a good director, a first-rate cameraman and a cutter who knew his job, a fairly dim actor could be made to look as though he was acting. In a stage production the part was given to a good-looking actor who could 'support' the star playing Rosalind. It may be that you are shortish, thick-set and have a north-country accent. Height – no problem. Some of our most distinguished actors are not even medium height. It does not stop them playing classical roles. It is the way they carry themselves that matters.

In the previous section we considered that since Orlando is making a very great fuss about not being 'bred well' it is probable that he has done what he can for himself. To be 'well bred' meant that you knew how to behave well in any social situation and for that you do not need to be bookish. So in spite of having lived with the servants and farm workers, he has probably watched Oliver and his friends and taken trouble with his appearance and manners. His doublet may be shabby – one of Oliver's cast-offs – but it is clean and well brushed. Accustomed to physical exercise of some kind and probably having taken part in all the games played by the servants around the estate, he is tough and he moves easily.

In approaching the part in a rehearsal situation you have accepted that the voice cannot come right unless the physicality is right. You will by this time have been given some preliminary instruction in voice and movement classes about posture, breathing, getting yourself centred and your weight properly disposed. All of this, though as yet probably very simple and basic, can help in finding the physicality of Orlando. He must be centred, otherwise he would not have the speed and flexibility to win the wrestling. (You will find more about the idea of CENTRE AND CENTRING in the third part of this book which is concerned with technique.) Posture? If I am centred that should be right. Breathing? Once again, if I am centred the breathing should not be difficult. Try applying all this to Orlando. Walk about, using what you have been told in class to explore the way Orlando moves.

Sometimes he is easy and relaxed where he has seen how a gentleman behaves and copied it. Sometimes, having to deal with a situation where a servant has done something wrong, he has used his strength and his natural authority to deal with it. He feels easy in his body and because of it, probably looks taller than he is. If you are tall and thin with a tendency to stoop then you will have to consider that a stoop usually suggests a scholarly type and that will not do for Orlando, but your stoop will most certainly have been noticed and commented on by voice and movement tutors and suggestions will have been made for work to improve your posture. Imagine situations where Orlando might have used his height as an asset, not as a liability. Young people often stoop because they are embarrassed at being taller than their fellows. Perhaps Orlando liked to show Oliver that he was the taller of the two!

So far as being good-looking is concerned, actors and actresses are far more frequently cast for an interesting personality than a handsome appearance. The pretty faces are doing modelling. The most wonderful performance of Rosalind I ever saw was given by an actress who was very plain and really too old for the part, but such was her magic, her exquisite speech, the marvellous freedom and grace of her movement and her sheer joyous spontaneity, that it was impossible to imagine anyone else playing the part. Beginner students often say, 'How can I act if I have to think about my voice and movement all the time? If I work in class at those things, won't they just gradually happen without my having to worry about them?' Yes, and no. You have to make use of your work imaginatively. To straighten your back and position your head correctly will almost certainly feel awkward at first, but what you have to keep exploring is the fact that Orlando would not feel this awkward with his physicality. You are re-educating your body to do what you want it to do at will and without trouble. Whatever you do, do not strain too much at first. Try standing and moving as Orlando. Speak a few of his lines while doing so. Then give it a rest. Your muscles will not adapt immediately to a different use. However, once accustomed to it, with the correct use of body comes a new freedom, not only physical but mental.

Now let us think of the physicality of Rosalind and Celia. I put them together because their background and upbringing will have been the same. They are spoken of as princesses, which may seem odd to us now since we are accustomed to princesses and princes being the children of the monarch. These girls each have a duke for a father and in our society the daughters of a duke are not referred to as princesses. However, in Shakespeare's day there were, over a great part of Europe, many large and small sovereign states whose rulers had the title of duke but whose children were spoken of as princes and princesses. These rulers were continually at war with one another, grabbing one another's territory and deposing one another, so the situation at the beginning of *As You Like It* seemed nothing out of the ordinary to an Elizabethan audience.

Students sometimes ask, 'Why do we have to be princes and princesses? Why can't we play them as ordinary people?' It is quite a sensible question. Such students are afraid of having to think too much about the exterior presentation and sometimes there is a feeling that the audience does not identify with characters in 'fancy dress' who lived so many years ago.

Let us start by getting rid of that word 'ordinary'. Just what do you mean by it? If you mean people like you and those in the group around you – are you ordinary? You would be far from pleased if I were to say that you were an ordinary lot. So let us start by substituting for 'ordinary' the word 'interesting'.

Why do we still play Shakespeare's plays? Because the people in them are interesting. Interesting and ordinary. That is to say, real people. Celia and Rosalind are 'ordinary' in as much as they are like many girls you know, but they are individuals with ideas and minds of their own, ideas which have been conditioned by their upbringing and education. So we have to understand and play both the real feeling of the characters and the social behaviour that has been imposed on them.

Nowadays the plays are rarely presented in the kind of costumes that Shakespeare's actors might have worn. Such costumes are hugely expensive and can, for the most part, only be afforded by film and television productions. Theatre directors not only find it less expensive to present the plays in modern dress but feel it may make them more accessible to a modern audience. Sometimes they will decide on period costumes but those of a time nearer to us than the doublet and hose worn by the men and the huge hooped skirts of Queen Elizabeth and her ladies. This, they feel, emphasises that Shakespeare does not belong to a particular period but is for all time.

I have always encouraged students to study and think about the clothes and customs of the period in which the play was written. This gives them a thorough knowledge of the character's background and enables them to adapt to the similarities and differences of another century. That way one discovers more about the characters and the way they behave as they do. In the case of Rosalind and Celia it is difficult for a present-day girl, accustomed to wearing jeans, shorts or a bikini, to imagine what it must have been like to have worn a long skirt and petticoats since she was a small child. To have been laced into a tight corset, to have worn such clothes all day and everyday, and then suddenly, because of a need for disguise, to get into a man's clothes – literally to find her legs, to find a physical freedom she had never experienced. For Celia, no heavy brocade skirt supported by a great padded petticoat, no stiff ruff around the neck, just a single linen undergarment, a free-flowing skirt of light material and a scarf around the shoulders.

The physicality of both girls would change completely from the way they would have been conditioned to behave in the court scenes and the way they can behave in the forest, where they retain their disguise since they are living in a shepherd's cottage. Rosalind has time to reveal herself to her father, indeed she meets him, but she does not reveal herself. Could it be that her father might be shocked and insist that she unpack a skirt from her baggage? Or does she stay as a boy because she wants to resolve the situation with Orlando? The court of Queen Elizabeth was noted not only for its splendour but for its decorum. The queen behaved with dignity, graciousness and charm. (There were moments when she was bad-tempered and outrageous, but these occasions were few considering the strains to which she was subjected in her lifetime, and she never behaved badly in public.) Those around her were expected to follow her example.

Rosalind and Celia would have been trained to behave like princesses. Even the Queen herself had a governess when she was a child who would have impressed upon her the standard of behaviour expected of her. So, in a way, if the director decides to do the play in modern dress it makes it more difficult for the actresses, not easier. In drama schools, students have – or should have – a good heavyweight practice skirt which can be worn at all rehearsals. Rosalind and Celia may have had something much more difficult to manage, but a good practice skirt is a great help to an actress. She can imagine that Rosalind may have worn something more restricting, but her own skirt with a petticoat under it, if she can find one, will give her the contrast – the feeling of freedom when she makes the change. So again, make an act of faith and say, 'I am Rosalind.'

Fortunately there is still a real-life queen we can look at. We can note the way our own Elizabeth walks in public – slowly, with great economy of movement and with dignity. So it is with Rosalind and Celia, trained by a dancing master to walk well: head up and free, shoulders relaxed, bust lifted (important that – those tight bodices were cut low and filled in with a transparent chemise).

The girls cast as Rosalind and Celia must look for at least three modes of behaviour. At the start, the two girls are alone. No need for courtly manners. The moment the Duke arrives with his entourage all is formality, dignity and awareness of social position. Celia is the most important lady present. She summons Le Beau and sends him on an errand. She and Rosalind do not go to Orlando, he must be summoned to come to them.

The girl playing Celia might think like this:

> Get into my practice skirt. If I have a wide elasticated belt I will wear
> that. It will help me to imagine constriction. Try it out at home. Walk
> around in it. Get centred, imagine myself a princess, but keep in mind

no affectations. Dignity, simplicity and awareness that I am the social superior of everyone around me – which means, if I am a nice person, I am nice to them (being careful not to be nicer to one than another because it might provoke jealousy). Today, any departure from good behaviour would mean a nasty press, but gossip has always been gossip so I must behave according to a code that can be generally approved. I must do nothing that might be open to misinterpretation.

There is quite a noticeable difference between the two scenes with Orlando. The second time they approach him they are much simpler in their behaviour. Rosalind is quite daringly straightforward when she tells him that he has wrestled well and overthrown more than his enemies. No wonder he is amazed to the point of being speechless. Rosalind gives him a chain from her neck. She is doing what the Duke should have done. An immediate reward for service was the custom. Orlando has won the match. He should have been rewarded. The usual reward in such circumstances was a purse of gold. When the person to be rewarded was the social equal of the donor then the gift was usually something from about the donor's person, a gold chain or a ring – something of value. Rosalind, in giving Orlando her chain, acknowledges him as her social equal. She has heard him say who his father was. Some Victorian actresses used to kiss the chain before giving it to Orlando, thus making it clear that it was a love gift. I find this sentimental and affected. Yes, Rosalind has fallen for Orlando, but in giving the chain she is behaving as a princess. When she comes back and asks, 'Did you call, sir?' she is behaving as a girl and there should be a distinction. If not, her line to Celia – 'My pride fell with my fortunes' – makes no sense.

Having though about the formal and less formal behaviour of Rosalind and Celia, consider their behaviour in the forest. On arrival they are exhausted, not used to walking long distances. Rosalind has fared better but then she probably has a comfortable pair of boots. Celia's over-large shoes may well have caused blisters. If I am playing Celia I am probably limping. I would not have known about the need to wear thick socks inside thick shoes! So there is a complete change in the way I am moving. Rosalind has been striding along, but suddenly she goes slack. Is the Forest of Arden not what it was cracked up to be? (Equate the feeling with a misleading travel brochure!)

'So this is the Forest of Arden!'

It would seem that we all flop down wearily. It is not what we expected. In a little while I, Celia, am going to say I like it, but I am feeling very tired right now. Rosalind and Touchstone exchange a few cracks and then a couple of natives appear who are discussing, of all things, love. This fascinates Rosalind and Touchstone, but it means that I can do something I could never have done at home – I can take off my shoes. What's more, I will. Listen to what is going on over there – still this talk of love! Is nobody hungry? They keep on about love so my body probably gathers itself into a listening position, a position of deep concentration. All this talk of love. I am listening for that magic word 'food'. If I do this truthfully I shall not distract from the scene because it will appear that I am deeply interested in what they are saying, which in a sense, I am. I am waiting for the mention of food. Consequently, when I do speak, the effect will be fun because the audience will have been led to expect from my intense concentration that I am about to contribute a word of wisdom about love. The intense thought expressed through my body will have created this expectation.

All these suggestions come from observation of myself and other people. Try them out for yourself. Do not imitate them, but try to find out the physical impulse for each one. In each case, you will find that the physical impulse happens before the spoken word. It may only happen a fraction of a second sooner, but it does happen – and with the intake of breath. Because this is something of which we are not conscious in our everyday lives. When we begin to think about it, it can be like so much else that we are learning – at first odd, even restricting. It can be worrying to realise that we have to do consciously what we normally do unconsciously.

Can we not just go on the stage and be natural? No, because acting is not natural. We are feeling and thinking not as ourselves, but as someone else. We have to discover what is natural to that person.

Physicality is not an easy subject to write about. It needs personal contact. It is the sort of thing that is worked out in class where the instinct of the actor can be guided by confirmation and suggestion from the tutor or the director. But it is as well to have something on paper as a reminder. Also, because time is so often against work in great detail, you must – if you are to be what I would call a 'dangerous actor' – be equipped to think for yourself.

Remember, 'Thy danger chiefly lies in acting well.' Acting is a physical process. Acting well involves using the body to express your innermost thoughts.

6 Gesture and movement

Everything we have just been thinking about is gesture. Everything you do on stage is a gesture. Don't do anything you don't mean to do.

Gesture is a word that is rather unfortunately misunderstood these days. It is all too often imagined as waving one's arms about in a somewhat affected manner. But a gesture really is a message. An audience sees an actress put her hand gently on another's arm, and, depending on how she does it, realises something of her feeling for that person. An actor strikes another and, depending on the violence of the action, communicates a certain level of hatred.

Gesture is the way people behave, what they do with their bodies day in and day out. It is what Desmond Morris calls 'body language'. So, no matter what character I am playing, I have to consider the body he inhabits and what he does with it. How does he stand, how does he walk, how does he sit, how does he move his body in relation to those around him? In a modern play, there are people in the world around to be observed, but in a classical play it is more difficult.

What do I mean by a classical play?

The dictionary definition begins well – 'of allowed excellence' but then it goes on to say, 'of the standard of Latin and Greek authors'. Most of us can join with Shakespeare in saying that we have little Latin and less Greek. But Shakespeare is a classical author, and so are the Jacobean playwrights and the Restoration playwrights, and so are Bernard Shaw and Oscar Wilde, and quite a few more.

Surely a classical play has to mean a play that has stood the test of time. A play that, presented today, has a quality that makes the audience recognise the characters and their predicaments as their own. Whether tragedy or farce, this recognition has to happen for a play to be considered a classic. It has to evoke the feeling, 'I am not alone.'

Of course, there are problems in what we call 'classical' plays. People do not behave as we do. The problem today's young actor has when approaching a classical part – one of Shakespeare's historical or Roman plays, perhaps – and studying, say, the character of Brutus or Cassius in *Julius Caesar* – is that he has no living human being to look at as an example.

The Elizabethans were not so troubled. For a start, not knowing much history they tended to assume the characters in the play wore the same clothes and behaved much as the people they saw around them. As for the portrayal of the kings and queens, princes and princesses that people Shakespeare's plays, ordinary people had sight of the great nobles almost every day. They saw the great nobles, lords and ladies, dressed magnificently according to their rank, riding or walking in the streets with their entourage of servants and followers; they saw their splendid clothes and the way they wore them.

The actors themselves, having played at court and in the great houses of the nobility, would have taken careful note of what they saw and heard. Shakespeare's company played at court. He would have had plenty of opportunity to note how people there behaved. If the characters in the plays presented were kings and courtiers, then he and the actors had to get it right, otherwise they would not be asked to play before the queen again! Getting it right was a commercial necessity: a performance at court was big money – something like a first-class orchestra could command nowadays.

In the television series, *I, Claudius*, the actors wore togas with great ease and naturalness, but the dialogue was modern English. An actor working on a scene from *Julius Caesar* has to think about the dialogue as well as what he might be wearing. Of course in many stage productions, particularly of this play, the director may decide to change the period and may even play it in modern dress. But when that happens there is another period to be studied and the play's relevance to that period. All Shakespeare's history plays deal with a political situation – the problem of good government.

A famous scene from *Julius Caesar* which deals with the political problem, but at the same time with a personal relationship which is going to develop and lead to the great quarrel scene at the end of the play, is the play's first meeting between Brutus and Cassius. Actors faced with it for the first time feel somewhat daunted. It looks as though it is all talk. There is no obvious movement except at the start when Brutus says, 'I'll leave you.' Cassius has two very long speeches. Those of Brutus are relatively short. So how might we discover the gesture and movement which will draw out the significance of the scene?

Well, what is the basic action? Cassius is trying to persuade Brutus to listen to him on a subject that he believes to be of great importance to both of them. Brutus seems disinclined to listen: he knows what Cassius wants to say but is as yet not willing to discuss it.

Brutus appears to be calm and reserved, Cassius more volatile and impetuous.

At no time do a couple of people talking politics stand immobile. So what are the actors to do? Too much restlessness or meaningless movement could distract the audience from the argument of the scene to which it is important that they give close attention.

Begin by taking what hints there are in the text.

> The scene starts as the two men enter with Caesar and his entourage. There is a short exchange in which Caesar speaks to Calphurnia and Antony and then has his attention caught by the Soothsayer, who bids him beware the Ides of March. Caesar derides the prophesy and moves off with his followers. Brutus and Cassius remain on stage alone. Brutus, it would seem, is lost in thought. Cassius, who has been about to leave, turns back to ask him if he will not be continuing on his way.
>
> All too often, the beginner student – feeling that since he is 'acting Shakespeare' a gesture is needed – will extend an arm at shoulder height with the palm of his hand flat in front as a salute to the departing Caesar. It does not dawn on the actor that he would never do that in real life. What he might do is make a slight move of his head, or shift his weight in that direction and then still be waiting for Brutus' response. Brutus' reply is brief and mechanical, so Cassius repeats his request, probably moving a step nearer to Brutus, who comes out of his absorption and, excusing himself courteously, starts to go. Cassius stops him.
>
> Look at the text. Brutus finishes a short speech of explanation with the short line, 'I'll leave you.' To which Cassius responds, 'Brutus, I do observe you now of late.'
>
> The printed text gives only a comma after Cassius speaking Brutus' name. But surely there would be a pause after 'Brutus' – enough time for Brutus to turn and for Cassius to take a step towards him and explain that he feels there to be an estrangement between them. Brutus, attending carefully, has time to consider his reply. If he has looked down when listening, his head will now come up as, having decided on his response, he speaks. If the actors feel the situation truly, their movements will sustain the pulse-beat of the verse.

Now Brutus turns, gives all his attention to Cassius and explains that of late there have been problems which he would rather not discuss, but apologises if his detachment has appeared coldness towards his friends. He may even give Cassius a reassuring touch on the shoulder as he says, 'Be you one.' The speech is carefully worded. The problems could be personal rather than political.

Cassius appears to see through the evasion. He might make a slight disbelieving movement. He goes on to say that because of Brutus' reserve he has refrained from mentioning important ideas of his own. He then makes an indirect and somewhat quaint approach by asking if Brutus can see his own face. It is so absurd that Brutus may feel forced to smile, turning a little way as he does so. The audience needs to see his face. Cassius has a habit of using language in this odd way and Brutus is indulgent and relaxes as he replies. What he does not realise is that Cassius uses his quirkiness to make Brutus drop his guard.

Then Cassius says, ''Tis just', and there is a half-line pause. The smile goes, replaced by apprehension. A total stillness. Cassius, also very still, drives the lines at Brutus, moving closer on the second part of the speech. Brutus, still without moving, probably takes a breath to reply to Cassius, but waits until he has finished speaking before rounding on him to ask, 'Into what dangers?' I think the stress must be on 'dangers'. The audience should feel it is the key word in the scene. Cassius may back away slightly, finding a position of strength before continuing. He is pressuring Brutus now, demanding his trust.

Then comes the clamour off-stage. Brutus turns and moves in the direction of the noise as though to see what is happening. Completely off guard, he speaks his thought aloud and Cassius sees his opportunity. He asks the great question and Brutus replies, honestly and sadly, then moves to Cassius. He tells him the conditions on which he is prepared to listen to what Cassius has to say.

Now Brutus has a long period of listening. What is the actor to do during it? Hardly necessary to say that he listens intently. But standing quite still and holding eye contact is not enough; and held too long, it begins to feel unreal, as indeed it would be. Both Cassius and the audience need to be aware that the speech is having an effect. When someone presents us with a problem one starts by looking at the speaker, then gradually the eyes turn away as the focus goes inward and one ponders on the content of what is being said. Cassius needs to make a sufficient pause at the end of the line 'endure the winter's cold as well as he' to realise that Brutus is caught, but not yet ready to respond, before deciding to tell the story that will illustrate his point.

Before starting, there is a second of relaxation. It is just a story, but it will explain what he means. Cassius smiles as he recalls the excitement of the incident, and of being young and strong. Brutus, drawn back to these days, also begins to smile. Even the idea of Caesar calling for help does no more than amuse him until Cassius pulls the situation up sharply with 'this man is now become a god.' Now Brutus understands, but he still cannot reply, so Cassius perhaps moves away in the pause after 'Caesar carelessly but nod upon him'. Then Cassius' indignation creates the need to relate the next incident; but this time there is no half-affectionate recollection of a boyhood escapade, but something remembered with contempt and bitterness. Brutus, lost in thought, still does not respond, and Cassius allows his indignation to explode. Before Brutus can respond there is another off-stage shout and Brutus again moves to look in that direction. He speaks another few words of apprehension.

Cassius scarcely notices the disturbance. His attention is all on Brutus and from a position of strength he goes into the attack. Brutus moves slowly and thoughtfully nearer. Cassius changes his tactic. He now says quietly that it is all our fault, we are to blame, we make no use of our opportunities. This is what Rome has come to and we let it happen. Then there is a reminder of Brutus' great ancestor who would as soon had the devil ruling in Rome as a king.

There is a half-line pause at the end of his speech, then Brutus looks at him and speaks. He knows what Cassius has in mind but he will not discuss it now. Possibly a slight move away before he decides to tell Cassius that he too finds the idea of Rome being anything but a republic intolerable. Cassius, with relief that he has succeeded so far, speaks the last lines of the scene and they turn to face the return from the games of Caesar and the rest.

It is of course preferable to work the movement out with the individual actors concerned. This is only an indication of what a couple of actors might think about when preparing the scene for a class in scene-work or rehearsal. Nevertheless, you will have realised that the actual movement in the Brutus-Cassius scene is very slight. But as well as speaking the words, the actors are feeling the impact of the situation physically, discovering the satisfaction of using the whole of themselves. A director working on the scene will have to consider the space in which he is working; the size and shape of the stage and the auditorium. If these are large he will have to help the actors to enlarge gesture and movement while keeping the truth of the impulse.

What we are talking about here is physical movement. Movement in speech – what is more often called rhythm – is also a major factor that has to be considered in rehearsal, and we shall be dealing with it in detail in SPEECH, the second part of the book. But the way the characters speak to each other clearly has an effect on their physical gesture and movement. The dialogue between Cassius and Brutus is flowing, evenly measured, blank verse. In the scene between Richard III and Lady Anne in the play *Richard III*, Shakespeare uses a different kind of dialogue. It is known as stichomythia and consists of quick, almost staccato-like, exchanges between the characters. Reading the text, one begins to realise that Richard is on the offensive and Anne the defensive, that his movements are a deliberate closing in on her and hers are evasive and far more instinctive. She moves because she dislikes and fears Richard, but as the extraordinary content of his words have their effect on her, she moves less and less until she is quite still as she listens to his long speech which begins, 'I would they were, that I might die at once,' to the moment he gives her his sword and she takes it. She twice makes an attempt to use it, but each time he speaks before the sword is near him – he did it all for her sake! After he tells her that he killed her husband, she lets the sword fall. Now he is close enough and she sufficiently bemused for him to take her hand and put the ring on it.

There will be much more movement in this scene than in the previous one, but a sensible actor and actress, preparing the work for class or preliminary rehearsal, can get some hints from the Brutus and Cassius scene.

Many actors do not sit when learning a part but like to walk around all the time. It is a good idea. Whether consciously or not, they are finding a rhythm for the character. They are certainly not feeling it to be physically static. They are probably making slight, instinctive movements in the direction of the thought, familiarising themselves with the space that they are going to use. It is a useful way to work. Good exercise, too.

Having looked in broad outline at what acting is, how to set about preparing a part, and the usefulness of considering the physicality of a character, let us now think in more detail about the idea of character. Acting is doing, expressing the innermost thoughts of the part you are playing. But before we can express anything, we have to know who the character is. In any case, what is character?

7 Knowing who you are: actor's background

Some students coming from a background with which they identify very strongly are worried that at drama school they will lose their identity.

They might worry that acquiring a standard English accent and learning certain social customs with which they are unfamiliar will lay them open to the accusation of becoming affected, of not being themselves. They might find living in two worlds – that of their home and upbringing, and that of their school – very difficult. It is natural for families and friends to feel that a change of accent, social manners and even style of dressing is alienating.

What it is important to understand is that it is not a social problem. Quite simply, one cannot expect complete understanding from those who have no experience of theatre, or why and how certain things happen in that world. It is simply no good trying to explain it. If you think about it, this is not something which happens only to someone like you. As one grows into one's teens and twenties one develops a highly critical attitude about speech, manners, morals, clothes, indeed about anything. You feel frowned on by parents, mocked at by siblings, pressured to conform to the prevailing fashion by your peers.

Parents are torn between wanting you to grow up and be yourself and the sadness of losing the child you were. This usually takes the form of complaints that these new friends of yours are changing you, that you are not being yourself. Most parents, however easy-going, have an idea of what they want their child to be, and have perhaps subconsciously guided you towards that. They try to interest you in what they like and away from what they do not like. In some families, this closeness extends to a very wide group – grandparents, uncles, aunts, cousins. They have strong tastes in common and can be very severe in the condemnation of outsiders of whom they do not approve. This tends to happen no matter what your social class, education or income. There comes a time when children, growing into adulthood, feel the need to get away, to explore the outside world, find out if the identity which has been imposed, albeit with the best intentions, is real or not.

Nowhere is this more apparent than in the young person who wishes to act. In the case of those coming from a successful theatrical background there may be strong backing or – if the parents have not been as successful as they had hoped – great anxiety. In the first case, you may feel the need to succeed as your parents have done; in the second, you may want to prove yourself as soon as possible. But whatever the background, since the actor must work on himself, certain changes are bound to happen. Must happen.

There is a Jewish saying that the child who pleases his parents most is the one who disobeys. Like all aphorisms, it is a partial truth. It could simply refer to the child who disobeys and is successful. Then we must ask in what way has he succeeded? Does it mean worldly success, or does it mean finding himself and his own way of life, however simple?

One must not be afraid of changes. It is not really you who are changing, but it can seem like that if your point of view changes – as it is bound to. If it did not, then you could not really become part of the adult world. You grow. If you are lucky, you never stop growing. But it is always you. Your 'character', complex and many-sided, may not always be easy for you to grasp at times, though others may find it alarmingly simple to categorise you.

It is your judgment that is going to matter in the long run. Practise using it. Watch what is happening around you and consider it. The life you observe and experience is the material you will use as an actor and an artist.

8 Knowing who you are: character's background

It is all important to make your entrance into a play knowing who you are.

Actors are sometimes less than good, even quite awkward, in a very small part because, having only a line or two to say, they find no indication in the text about the kind of character who speaks those lines. They know that they must not distract from the work of more important actors, but they feel unreal and do not quite know how to contribute to the scene. The director is far too busy to do more than give them a general idea of what he wants and let them get on with it. They may even be told, 'just be yourself,' which can be even more frightening.

This is when the actor must get his imagination working. I can still remember a student of years back playing a one-line bit in *Trelawney of the Wells*. He had a single entrance as the stage-doorkeeper who had to interrupt the director in rehearsal to say that there was someone at the stage-door who wished to speak to him. The actor had clearly worked out that since the doorkeeper did not send the visitor up immediately, but came himself to ask if he should, the man must have had doubts about the propriety of the situation. The actor had made himself up to look like such a man. He was dressed quite formally. He had a drooping moustache, carefully brushed hair and pince-nez on a ribbon – an image of respectability. When he spoke there was just a hint of disapproval. On being told to send the visitor up, the disapproval increased as he made his significant exit. He had not only given a brief but complete sketch of a character, but he had added to the situation in the play. This was a real theatre with a real doorkeeper who had his standards. His use of an old-world disapproval added to the fact that the situation on stage was unusual and he minimised any anticipation on the part of the audience that a long-lost lover was about to reappear. This constituted a very tactful and intelligent piece of acting.

In *Hamlet*, the soldier Francisco only ever appears once – in the first few moments of the play. As an actor, he may have other duties – playing another small part and perhaps understudying, but this may be his only speaking part. Superficially, the scene is quite ordinary, merely the changing of sentries on the battlements of a castle. But it is not an ordinary night because on the previous night these men have seen a ghost. The ghost of the late king. Although there is no mention of this until after the entrance of Horatio and Marcellus, there is something unusual about the exchange between Bernardo and Francisco. To start with, it is not the sentry on watch who gives the challenge, but the man who is coming to replace him. The opening therefore has a tension, with both men carefully hiding their nerves.

Then Francisco has a speech of three phrases: 'For this relief much thanks' – nothing in that; ''Tis bitter cold' – gives us the atmosphere we need; then, 'I am sick at heart.' What is wrong? He has had a very quiet guard but he is thankful to be relieved and he is 'sick at heart'. Why? What kind of man does that suggest? Well, the actor could think up something that would satisfy him, such as that his wife was ill. But that would be outside the play and would take the actor's attention outside it. Bernardo inquires as to whether the watch has been a quiet one: it would seem that the unease is something that they both share. At this moment in the action of the play there is only one thing that could make a man 'sick at heart'. Suppose he has been a devoted admirer of the late king. Then the appearance of the ghost might make him apprehensive that all is not well in Denmark – he does not like what he suspects, he is glad to go off watch. From that, you can create for yourself the kind of man who would have such a response to the situation. Remember, play what the character does.

Francisco's remark, 'I am sick at heart' has to do with a strangeness both men are experiencing here and now, but about which they are being as cautious and casual as possible. There are things unspoken between them. A taut and real situation; enough, in spite of the economy of the dialogue, to enable actors to play the mystery of the scene, and to work out for themselves characters who would react in the way they do. All the audience needs to know is there in the text, but the actor has to imagine the background for himself – something of the life the character has lived before the play starts. The actor has to feel secure that he is somebody, not just someone spouting lines.

But suppose that you are playing a secretary with one line, the corny classic, 'Here are the papers you asked for, sir.' What to do about that? Well, again, pay attention to background.

What kind of office? What kind of boss? A secretary will reflect her surroundings. Is she a perfectly groomed glamour girl in the office of a high powered tycoon, or is she a scruffy teenager in a sleazy back-street agency? Is she a somewhat older woman who pretty well runs the office but is so discreet as to be almost invisible? Does her attitude to 'the papers' mean anything? Does the situation warrant a sly look at the boss? Or is she totally indifferent, in which case, get in as quietly as possible and leave with the intention of finishing the cup of coffee getting cold in the outer office.

If you are only walking on in a crowd, invent a character for yourself, work out why you have to join in the booing or cheering or whatever. Always remember, get your idea from what the character does, from how he reacts to the situation in which he is involved. Most importantly, make sure that whatever you invent contributes to the scene and does not distract from it.

Doing something in a scene which distracts the attention of the audience is a sign of a selfish and untruthful actor.

9 Character and decisions

What is a character?

In dramatic terms, a character is the full sum of his actions and reactions. No character exists in a vacuum. A character exists in his relation to other people, in the effect they have on him and on the action he takes as a consequence of that effect.

If you examine any of the great Shakespearian soliloquies you will find that a character is examining the effect of other people's opinions or actions, real or imagined, on himself, arguing with himself – with his inner self – and making a consequent decision about his own action.

Hamlet's first soliloquy (I ii 129-159) illustrates this very clearly: 'O, that this too too solid flesh would melt.' He is reacting strongly against his mother's conduct; he continually tells himself not to think about it, and in the end he decides, 'I must hold my tongue'.

Benedick's soliloquy at the beginning of Act II, Scene iii of *Much Ado About Nothing* is a reaction to the discovery that his friend, Claudio, is in love. This prompts him to ask if it is possible that he himself could ever fall in love. Not, he decides, unless there should be a woman with all the qualities he would want. No, says his inner self, it is not likely.

But after overhearing talk between Claudio, Don Pedro and Leonato, he has another soliloquy. He now questions what he feels about Beatrice. His inner self tells him that she is desirable and he decides that he will be 'horribly in love'. A situation has been considered; other people have intervened, as a result of which Benedick decides that he can love.

This is what we mean when we talk of a character developing: the person has been changed by events or people, makes different decisions, is no longer quite the same; but of course his reactions are the character's, and the character's alone; he has not become someone else. Both Hamlet and Benedick react to the evolving situations in which they are caught up because of what they know and feel – Hamlet about the Queen, and Benedick about Beatrice – but as they change they are no less distinctly Hamlet and Benedick. The decisions they make in response to their changing circumstances reveal the very essence of their character.

So when you are preparing your part, think in terms of being affected by other people and making consequent decisions. Find the conflict between self and inner self.

We have started talking quite a lot about **decisions**. Some actors talk of 'making choices'. It means the same thing. Decisions, or making choices, play a very important role in the dangerous art of acting and creating a character. Decisions are of two kinds: the **actor's decision** and the **character's decision**. In the first, you, the actor, know the whole story; in the second, you, the character, only know that part of the story of which you have been made aware.

In his first soliloquy Hamlet only knows that his mother has married, very hastily, a man he detests. If he does suspect that Claudius has killed his father there is no inkling of it until the ghost makes the accusation. Even so, he is not certain until after the play scene. Of course, the actor knows, and, perhaps unfortunately, many of the audience nowadays are in the know. Imagine what the very first performance must have been like when the play was new. There is a level on which *Hamlet* is a wonderful detective story.

Consider *Romeo and Juliet*. Romeo does not know, at the beginning of the play, that he will fall in love with Juliet. When he goes to the Capulet ball, he is in love with another girl. Juliet does not know that she will meet and fall in love with Romeo. She is expecting to meet, and probably fall in love with, Paris. Sometimes, actors spoil their performances by being too conscious of how the story ends. Because a character kills himself at the end, they tend to play melancholy all the way through. However, Shakespeare's characters are seldom melancholics by nature – not even Hamlet: look at what Ophelia says of him, and at the way he jokes with Rosencrantz and Guildenstern before he realises that they have been brought to Elsinore to spy on him. On the whole, Shakespeare's characters reveal a great desire to enjoy life.

The character's decisions are all in the text. The actor's decisions are arrived at by a study of the text and by an awareness of his relationship with fellow actors.

If the character decides to kill himself, the action and reason for this decision are in the text. But decisions about the physicality of the action – just how he meets death, where and how he shall fall – all these are made by the actor who will try to find ways that he believes will be right for that character.

The interior action is in the text and is immutable. The reason for the action is in the text and must be translated by the actor into a feeling of his own.

The actor's decision is mutable. It concerns how the action is performed – and this may be done differently every rehearsal until the best way seems to have been discovered. If the search is conducted truthfully, it will be different with each actor who plays the part, different in every production of the play.

So, even at the first reading of a play, look for the actions of the other characters, their effect on you and the decisions you, the character, make as a result of those actions.

10 Living the part

Students frequently ask, 'How can I be myself and somebody else at the same time?'

Peter Brook, when asked if he thought that an actor really lived a part, replied sensibly that this was not possible. He pointed out that were it so, Oedipus would have to put his eyes out before playing the last scene and, however dedicated the actor, he might not be willing to do that! Anyway, how could he play the following night, or ever again for that matter?

So why do actors talk of 'living the part' and why are they praised for doing so? What happens is that we develop a skill in self-hypnosis: while we are acting we believe we are someone else; at the same time, spectators 'suspend disbelief' and while they are watching share the same kind of deep concentration that the actor achieves. Living the part is a phrase we use for describing total imaginative commitment. Stanislavski, in using the phrase, points out that we have no command over the subconscious. We use imagination in the same way as children playing a pretend game. Like them, we believe that we are the character.

A child does not monitor his own performance. But the professional actor, like every other artist, has a monitor. A painter reaches a stage when he will move back from his painting and look at it. He may spend a very long time looking at it before he goes back to take up the palette and brushes. This process is likely to be repeated again and again. (Think of Leonardo da Vinci spending hours just looking at *The Last Supper* or Michelangelo brooding over those last great sculptures. They were monitoring their work and at the same time involved in it.)

No analogy, and no comparison, is exact. But judging by descriptions of performances by eighteenth and nineteenth century theatre critics, it would seem that the attitude to acting then was very different from ours today. The idea of actors working together as a group, sharing ideas of the play, and not trying to upstage one another and hog the limelight, would have appeared very odd. It was every actor's ambition to be a star. But the star system did not have entirely negative results. Indeed, it was fervently believed that star status was achieved by working for truth and integrity; and to judge from the contemporary descriptions – if what was written about those great performers was true – it worked.

How did they do it? Perhaps by what Shakespeare calls a 'forcing of the soul'. Sometimes there was a partner. A great actor or actress finds stimulus from a great partner. There must have been discussions and critical insight from both. There were performers whose egos were so great that no competition of any kind was allowed. And of course, no criticism. (This is a phenomenon, it must be admitted, which is not unknown in our own day.) Looking back as far as Macready it would seem that a great role was worked out in a series of effects. These effects could be applauded by the audience much as an aria is applauded even now in opera. The performer would acknowledge the applause and sometimes give an encore. That sort of thing you could prepare on your own. Macready would work very hard indeed on an effect before trying it on an audience. If it did not work he would either scrap it or work to improve it. It was a completely self-conscious operation.

The spread of Stanislavski's teaching – which is so much about the research an actor does into the truth and reality of the character and of the absolute necessity of actors working together as a group – has to a great degree eliminated the selfish performance-orientated actor. Indeed, as much as anybody, it is the director who has become the star. This has, of course, led to abuses as bad as under the old actor-manager system.

It is possible for someone with no training or knowledge of the theatre to become a director, and those who have had some sort of training – which may consist of no more than a few weeks on a summer course – may try, by imposing some far-fetched idea on a play, to get reviews for 'originality'. They then move on to do the same damage to plays and actors elsewhere. These people have usually only one quality. They have the gift of the gab! But they have an excess of it. They talk themselves into work. They are dangerous people. If their production is a failure they will blame the actors, if a success they will scoop the glory, even though, in desperation, the actors have got together and done it themselves.

The modern actor is no Macready. However, we must not decry Macready. In many respects he was a very great man of the theatre. The actor can never, must never, dispense entirely with his monitor. There are times when, like Macready, you must be your own monitor. (In my classes we have a habit of referring to the monitor as 'Charlie'.) In the early stages of rehearsal the actor can be his own monitor, but the director, if he is a really good one, will gradually take over the role of monitor and leave the actor free to invent, imagine, believe. He may give the actor some fairly stiff notes, but if a rapport has been established and the director is aware of the actor's creative process and his sensitive inner self that may be protected by a prickly exterior, all will be well.

The great eighteenth century actress Sarah Siddons was renowned for her performance as Lady Macbeth. Here is her answer to the question of living the part: 'When a part is first put before me for studying, I look it over in a general way to see if it is in Nature, and if it is I am sure it can be played... Whenever I was called upon to personate the character of Constance [*King John*] I never, from the beginning of the play to the end of my part in it, once suffered my dressing room door to be closed, in order that my attention might be constantly fixed on those distressing events which, by this means, I could plainly hear going on upon the stage – the terrible effects of which progress were to be represented by me... In short, the spirit of the whole drama took possession of my mind and frame, by my attention being incessantly riveted on the passing scenes.' Later, she had occasion to remark: 'Belvidera [*Venice Preserved*] was hardly acting last night; I felt every word as if I were the real person, and not the representative.'

What is to the point here is that she is speaking of a single performance of a part she played frequently. Even for a genius of the stature of Sarah Siddons, the greatest actress of her day, total identification was not something that happened every performance – although Siddons must have come as near as anyone to achieving it. Her powers of concentration were so complete that the emotions which possessed her continued for several hours after a performance. It is said that when she was playing Mrs Haller in *The Stranger*, Siddons never stopped crying until she reached home, and her daughter Sally wrote, 'My mother cries so much at it all that she is always ill when she comes home.'

Garrick, that other great actor of the time, could joke easily between the acts of his most tragic roles, so you might assume he was superficial and frivolous, but this is what he wrote about a famous actress of his time in a letter to a friend:

> Your dissection of her is as accurate as if you had opened her alive; she has everything that art and understanding, with great natural spirit, can give her. But then I fear (and I only tell you my fears and open my soul to you) the heart has none of those instantaneous feelings, that life-blood, that keen sensibility, that bursts at once from genius, and like electrical fire, shoots through the veins, marrow, bones and all of every spectator. Madame Clairon is so conscious and certain of what she can do that she never, I believe, had the feelings of the instant come upon her unexpectedly; but I pronounce that the greatest strokes of genius have been unknown to the actor himself, until circumstances and the warmth of the scene, have sprung the mine as it were, as much to his own surprise as that of the audience. Thus, I make a great difference between a great genius and a good actor.

I do not think Stanislavski could have put it better!

blueprint a modern classic

Mrs Linde *A Doll's House*

Let us look at preparing a part from a more modern play – a classic play, but written in the naturalistic prose style of the late nineteenth century.

The dramatic influence of Strindberg, Chekhov and Ibsen has lasted to the present day. They wrote plays which have as their protagonists, not kings and princes, but ordinary men and women leading ordinary lives, concerned with the quality of those lives. They do not live at court, but in houses. They use speech which, though edited and compressed to give the greatest possible expression to what is being said, sounds like the speech we use every day.

I am deeply concerned not to tell you how to play a part, but what to look for and how to make your own blueprint, so that you can prepare for yourself. Remember to take into reheasal your observation, imagination and related experience. And remember that your fellow actors will have conceptions of your character as well as their own. There will be need for much understanding of their points of view and of a clear communication of yours – which is why a blueprint is so useful. When making a blueprint, there are four areas of information to draw on in the preparatory exploration of a part:

1) the play as a whole – understanding my part in it
2) my actions in each scene – 'What do I do?'
3) the reasons for my actions – 'Why do I do it?'
4) considerations about movement

Mrs Linde is not the principal character in *A Doll's House*. But as Nora is regarded as a star part and there are accounts of performances given by great actresses of the past, there is (as always for a young and inexperienced actress) a certain feeling of apprehension, of being measured against a great part and great performances of the past. It is difficult in these circumstances to see Nora simply as the human being Ibsen intended.

Mrs Linde is one of those characters who are usually referred to as supporting parts and though there are special awards to be won in such roles, one hardly ever hears an actress expressing a great desire to play one. Their qualities and problems are overshadowed by the leading parts, but that does not mean that they are dim and uninteresting, just there to give support. In the case of Mrs Linde, she is very important in the context of the play.

1) The play as a whole – understanding my part in it

You will of course read the play through carefully and more than once before starting work on the part. It is good to ask oneself why the character is in the play. Is Christine Linde there as a contrast to Nora? Yes, of course, that is one reason. She is a contrast to Nora not merely in social manners, but in life experience.

Think back for a moment to the material explored in *As You Like It*. Is there anything in common between the two plays? Ibsen is dealing with a very different world. Nora and Christine are not wealthy and beautiful princesses, but middle-class women living in a small, enclosed provincial world. What of the major theme in both plays? Rosalind, wildly in love, disguises herself as a boy and, free of the conventional ideas of what a truly loving relationship should be, challenges Orlando to rid himself of some of these conventional ideas he may have picked up – for instance, that it is the done thing to write poems in which the beloved is compared to every wonderful goddess or glamorous woman who has ever existed. Rosalind seems to be saying, 'Yes, it is wonderful, but you are not going to live with someone like that.' Passionately in love, she is still sensible and realistic.

Nora lives, not in the Forest of Arden, but in a flat in a provincial town in Norway during the latter part of the nineteenth century, yet unlike Rosalind, she does not appear have as good an understanding of the real world. She is happy to play the image which the men of her period (first her father and then Helmer) have imprinted on her. Rosalind knows herself pretty well, but has to discover the real self of the man she loves. Nora has to discover her real self. By contrast, Christine Linde, treated roughly by life, knows who she is and what she needs and is utterly realistic about the possibilities of what life has to offer her.

Both women in *A Doll's House* have experienced marriage. Nora believes hers to be entirely successful because her husband loves the image of herself that she is content to play. Mrs Linde admits that she married a man she believed to be wealthy in order to look after her family. When he died she discovered that he was not a rich man. He left her nothing, 'not even memories', because the marriage was loveless and without children.

So the actress starting work on the part can say:

> I have had a life of difficulty and hard work. I gave up the man I loved because marriage to a wealthy man meant that I could help my mother and brothers who were left penniless on the death of my father. For some reason, I did not, or could not, explain this to the man I really cared for and he was left to believe that I had jilted him for the other man's wealth. On my husband's death it transpired that he had no money and I had to turn to work – 'a small shop, then a small school, and so on. The last three years have seemed like one long working-day' – but I am dignified and courageous. There is only one moment of bitterness, for which I apologise at once, and I admit to being proud of having helped my mother and brothers as I did.

My feeling for Nora? It would seem that I find her unchanged from school-days, just as warm-hearted and full of gaiety, as mischievous and as unaware of the darker side of life. This last aspect of her character begins to worry me and – when she confides in me what she has done – causes me real concern. It is clear that we are really fond of one another and though life has treated us differently we have one great quality in common which allows us to understand each other: we care deeply for other people and feel a responsibility towards them. As the play progresses, I should perhaps speak more and more to Nora as to a beloved younger sister, especially when I find out the truth of her situation and try to persuade her that she must confide in her husband. Nora has a happy way of disregarding good advice that has always made it impossible to be really angry with her. Do I feel that Helmer will be angry with her? No, surely he will see her basic innocence and help her out of the situation. Anyway, because I have met Krogstad again and discovered that he is the man to whom Nora owes money, I feel sure that I can persuade him not to betray her. I go in search of him, but he is out of town and will not be back until tomorrow – the night of the dance.

I leave a note asking him to call at the Helmers' flat as soon as he returns. In the scene that follows we come to an understanding: we see how the mistakes of the past have affected us and realise we should build on that mutual understanding to create a future for ourselves. It follows from this, and I am insistent here, that we must let things take their course so that Helmer and Nora may come to a similar understanding. (This would seem to be a prologue to the final great scene in the play between Nora and Helmer.) Battered by experience of loneliness and poverty, we can both face reality and the fact that our experiences may have prepared us for a life together.

My importance in the play, then, is to demonstrate that I have managed to do what I set out to do – in the face of difficult circumstances. The example of my courage and ability to fend for myself must influence Nora in her decision to leave Helmer.

That is information from study of the play as a whole, from which I understand better my part in it. Now for the second stage of the blueprint.

2) My actions in each scene – 'What do I do?'

The philosopher Henri Bergson in his essay on 'Laughter' described action as being in exact proportion to the feeling that inspires it. Our sympathy – or our aversion – gradually passes along a line running from feeling to action. The two are closely linked – what we do (our actions) and the reasons for doing them (our feelings). So let us look at Mrs Linde's first appearance in Act I. What are her actions?

This is a little more difficult to answer than in *As You Like It*. For Mrs Linde, the actions seem clouded in conversation. We may well think that there is nothing to be done but sit and listen to Nora. Certainly, for the most of the scene Nora is explaining herself and her situation. I, Mrs Linde, am frequently making only slight and tentative reactions. Why? Because what she has to tell me is so unusual. Most of the time I am listening to her. When I do initiate an action and tell her something of myself, she quickly makes it an occasion for a further revelation of her own situation, which at this moment she believes to be utterly joyous, but which I begin to see could be fraught with danger for her.

1. I initiate my first action after I am shown in by a maid: since Nora does not recognise me I speak first. (I must remember to go through the background of the character. Ask myself what I expect to find in my social background and education.)

2. Nora is immediately warm and welcoming. She is concerned that I look paler and thinner. She remembers that I am now a widow and is concerned for what she thinks must be my grief. She apologises for not having written. I tell her I understand. There are a few lines of interchange. Nora expresses her concern that I have been left badly off – not even children and memories? With my response, 'It sometimes happens', Ibsen gives a very helpful direction. As I speak the line, I stroke Nora's hair. A gesture that shows my old affection for her, my realisation that she does not understand and my lack of self-pity. She contrasts my situation with her own by speaking of her three lovely children. Then immediately – perhaps feeling that she is being tactless – demands to know more about me.

3. Here the scene changes. I am not here to renew an old friendship, fond as I am of Nora. The difference in our circumstances would make that difficult. I am a working woman and she is comfortably married. When she, with undoubted concern, asks to be told about myself, I tell her that I want first to hear about her. Almost immediately, in her happiness and her exuberance, she confirms what I had heard, that her husband has been made manager of the bank. I encourage her to talk of him. In fact, in spite of her resolution to talk about me she cannot resist talking about what has happened, chatting on about how wonderful it will be to have 'heaps and heaps of money'.

4. This provokes me to comment wryly that to have enough would be good. I am also amused to recollect that Nora was a spendthrift at school.

5. Surprisingly – and here is another change of direction – Nora protests that she too has had to work. She talks of the usual odds and ends of needlework by which a woman in her position can make a little 'pin money', and

she hints at something else. She goes on to tell me how hard her husband worked and how the overwork brought on a breakdown: they had to go south for a whole year. This cost a tremendous amount of money.

6. Wistfully, I tell her one is lucky to have money for such emergencies. Nora explains that it came from her father, who was also ill at the time. Her husband is well again now.

7. I inquire about the doctor I met in the hall. (This is the start of a new section.) Nora dismisses that quickly: he is not their doctor but a personal friend. Now she insists on knowing about my affairs.

8. The moment has come where it is possible to tell her what my life has been and why it is important for me to find work. Nora is sympathetic, but with her limited experience of life she fails to understand my need and suggests I should take a holiday!

9. For the first time I am exasperated with her. I tell her I have no father to give me money to go away.

10. Nora is upset and I apologise, explaining that in my position it is difficult not to be bitter. I then reveal that when I heard of her husband's appointment I was delighted, not merely for her, but for myself!

11. Nora realises that I perhaps mean Helmer could help me, and is immediately delighted and confident that she can persuade him to do so.

12. I thank her and comment on her kindness, when she cannot imagine the difficulties that are experienced by people like myself.

13. Here is a another turning-point in the scene. Nora cannot resist telling me that she has had to work for others and can be proud of it. She goes so far as to say that it was she who saved her husband's life and she who found the money for the trip abroad. She is apparently light-hearted about it, which causes me some bewilderment and makes me question her with some concern. No, she has not won it in the sweepstake! And, of course, she could not have borrowed it! She even suggests in fun that she might have been given it by an admirer! However, I take this seriously and ask with real concern if she has not been imprudent. She laughs at the idea and goes on to say that somehow she did borrow the money and has been working in secret ever since to pay it off. It has been difficult, and it would seem that she has not paid off much, but she is highly delighted with what she has done, and now that Helmer will be getting such a high salary, she will be able to pay it off immediately. I interrupt with questions and exclamations

of concern while she pours it all out, but before I can get from her exactly how she got the money, the doorbell rings and I suggest that I had better go. The maid enters and speaks to Nora, who inquires who it is. Catching a glimpse of a man at the door, and hearing his voice, I move away. As soon as he has gone I ask Nora who it is. The answer is Krogstad.

14. Another turning-point. I ask questions about Krogstad. I explain that I used to know him many years ago. I have heard that he is a widower. Nora says that he has been left with several children. I ask a rather strange question about how he earns his living. Nora dismisses it casually, but before I can make any further inquiry Dr Rank enters from Helmer's study, saying he wants to talk to Nora.

15. Nora introduces him and he says pleasantly that he has often heard of me from her and asks if he did not pass me on the stairs? I reply that I find stairs difficult. He inquires if I am ill. I tell him that I have been overworking myself. He presumes that I have come to town for recreation. I tell him I have come to look for work. He inquires if that is a good cure for overwork. I tell him one must live. His comment is somewhat cynical and Nora intervenes with her usual lightness, but this provokes another cynical comment from Rank. Everyone wants to live as long as possible, even the morally diseased – one of whom is with Helmer now – and even he, Rank points out, has been insisting that he must live. Rank thinks it is wrong that such people are frequently helped and given good positions while the healthy-minded are left out in the cold.

16. I say that it is the sick who are most in need of care. Rank reproves me strongly for a sentiment that is turning society into a sick-house. Before I have time to protest, Nora bursts out laughing. Rank asks why she is laughing and if she knows what society really is. She says she neither knows nor cares, but does want to know if her husband has power over all the employees at the bank. Rank questions the reason she finds that amusing, but she laughs it off and offers him a macaroon. When he exclaims that he thought they were forbidden, she tells him that I gave them to her!

17. Nora starts to be frivolous in a way that I probably remember well from school. (It is important to realise that Nora's gaiety is natural to her: it has become her way of dealing with the people in her life; and finding it charming, they have refused to accept any other aspect of her personality.) There is certainly a sense of amusement as Helmer enters. Having satisfied herself that Krogstad has gone, Nora introduces me to her husband, who is immediately polite, presuming that I am an old school friend. I reply conventionally that we have known each other since then. Nora, continuing with her sparkling manner, tells him that I have taken a long journey just to

see him. Before either of us can question or refute this, she goes on to tell him how clever and capable I am, flattering him and impressing him with my desire to work for a clever man. Helmer is used to her exaggeration and probably amused by it, but, realising that I probably am capable, manages to get in a couple of questions as to my qualifications before Nora bursts in again as though it were all fixed up. Helmer manages to tell me that I have come at a fortunate time, but that he cannot talk further today. I thank him. He and Rank prepare to leave and I gather my things. To Nora's query, I say I must find a room. Nora, helping me with my cloak, apologises for not being able to have me to stay, but presses me to come back in the evening. I go out with Helmer and Rank.

3) The reasons for my actions – 'Why do I do it?'

Ibsen gives a direction that when I (as Mrs Linde) enter, I seem timid and dejected, but it seems to me (as the actress) to be misleading. My general behaviour is naturally uncertain at the start – Nora does not immediately recognise me – and I have come to ask a favour, which is probably something I dislike having to do. But there is something in my behaviour later in the scene and in my actions in the latter part of the play, both with Nora and with Krogstad, that suggests that although I may have had a difficult life, I am a woman of strong character. In preparing myself for this interview, would I not then have thought to have appeared as dignified as possible? Nora's warmth eases the situation. Going through the actions as listed, most of them seem self-explanatory. What I need to look for are the moments when the scene changes direction.

The first of these occurs in (3) when Nora asks to know about me and I say I must first hear about her, and she cannot resist telling me first of her husband's appointment. That is good news for me, although I make no comment on it yet. I do remark somewhat wryly that it would be delightful to have enough for one's needs. Nora, not noticing what I have said, goes on to talk about heaps and heaps of money. I laugh at her for being the same spendthrift she was at school. Then Nora tells me that they have not by any means always been well off. Both Helmer and she have had to work! When I show surprise that she should have worked, she says that she did odds and ends of crochet and needlework. She hints at 'other things' and tells me how much the trip cost, which provokes from me the comment that it is nice to have money in emergencies. I am wondering how bits of ladylike fancy work could have yielded two hundred and fifty pounds! She answers my unspoken thought by saying they had it from her father. But if her husband is now quite well, why has the doctor called? I may think, if Helmer is not quite fit, can he take up a responsible position at the bank?

But Nora is off again about Dr Rank, calling him a close friend of the family, who visits at least once a day. Then there is a burst of joy and then one of self-reproach because she has not inquired about me. She asks the obvious question – if I did not love my husband why did I marry him? My answer is simple and straightforward. I say that because of my responsibilities I did not think myself justified in refusing him. Nora considers this and gives her approval, which releases me from the reserve I have so far shown. I now confide in her with total freedom. I have to explain to her what my life has been because, in spite of her sympathy, it is not easy for her to understand. The suggestion that I should have a really good holiday provokes my one moment of bitterness – and something near self-pity – for which I apologise, before revealing that my visit was not just to renew our acquaintance. Another woman might have been a little cool at this, but Nora is delighted to be able to help me. She will deal with her husband for me! I find this touching as she can know so little of the burdens and troubles of life.

This is the turning-point as it causes Nora to tell me that I look down on her for not having had to work so hard for others. She tells me I am proud of what I have done. To which I tell her I think I have a right to be. (I do not have a right to much else, but a firm hold on my dignity makes me refrain from pointing that out.) Nora tells me that not only do I have a right to be proud, but so does she. It was not her father who gave her the money to go Italy. She found the money!

Astonished, I ask her did she win it – she could not have borrowed it without her husband's consent. Nora jokes about having been given it by an admirer, but I begin to be concerned, a concern which probably grows as I hear more of her situation and what she did, especially as she has never told her husband. Her response to my query as to how much she has managed to pay off shows a lamentable lack of business sense and she misleads me mischievously with further talk of a rich admirer. She laughs at my concern and rattles on about what a good time she and Helmer will have with the money. I am probably shaking my head at her, but laughing all the same, when the doorbell rings.

I suggest leaving (I am shabbily-dressed, and so not quite acceptable socially). When I hear Krogstad's voice, I move to the window. I am not quite sure that it is he, and anyway I do not want to meet him in front of Nora.

After he has gone out I ask who it was and tell her that I used to know him years ago. I cautiously ask a few questions about him. Nora is evasive, but before I can press her, Dr Rank enters.

How does he impress me? Clearly a distinguished man with good manners, he seems also to be caring: when he hears I am not entirely well he too suggests a holiday. He makes a slight joke when I say that I have come for work. Perhaps I am sufficiently well-mannered to smile slightly when I reply that one must live. His cynical response provokes remonstrance from Nora and further cynicism from him about the morally diseased, giving as an example someone who is with Helmer now. Of course, it is Krogstad. I have to listen to Rank's forceful opinions about people like Krogstad. When I protest, quite strongly, I am told that, like many others, I am sentimental on the subject.

Before I have time to respond, Nora laughs. She is delighted that her husband will have power over all bank employees, but diverts the conversation by offering macaroons, naughtily saying that I gave them to her. She continues with light-hearted nonsense until Helmer enters.

What do I think of Helmer? Good-looking, attractive, well-mannered. Just the sort of husband for Nora. He has authority. He will be a good bank manager. Now Nora is already telling him that I have called to see him because I am wonderfully clever at book-keeping and I want to work for a really clever man. While she talks on, Helmer is probably summing me up, because he starts questioning me as a possible employee. He seems to respect me. We are probably smiling at one another in a mutual feeling for Nora's warmth and exuberance. When I go out with the two men I am obviously in a much happier mood than when I entered. I think I may like Helmer.

4) Considerations about movement

Women of this period wore corsets. I must remember that in rehearsal. It was not only bad manners for women to slouch but very uncomfortable. If I can get a corset to wear for rehearsal it would be very helpful. If not, find a wide belt and have it as tight as possible.

Long skirt, of course, my practice skirt. Petticoats too, if I can get any. Do my hair up. Hat? It is mid-winter in Norway. A small fur hat would be good. A coat, a small muff. Of course, gloves – rather old, shabby gloves – perhaps darned. The darning will not be seen by the audience, but it will remind me that I am not well off. Boots, as well. These are all the things it would be good to have for rehearsal, and the kind of thing one uses in a workshop performance.

When I am welcomed and seated by Nora I would take off my gloves and loosen, if not take off, my scarf and coat. Sit straight. Arrange my skirt. Smooth it. All these things would be habitual to a woman like me, not even thought about. So I need to practise them in rehearsal to make them seem completely natural.

I might consider the idea that Mrs Linde, if she had money, would be quite elegant. As it is, her clothes will be old, but well cared for. It was important to try to keep up appearances in that society and I can see that it is important, because Helmer, looking at me, sees someone who might be an asset at the bank.

In a fully costumed production, the dress designer and the wardrobe mistress will produce clothes for you, but it is a good idea to have some notion of how you need to look and to have studied the costumes of the period.

speech

Speak the speech, I pray you, as I pronounc'd it to you, trippingly on the tongue; but if you mouth it, as many of our players do, I had as lief the town-crier spoke my lines. Nor do not saw the air too much with your hand, thus, but use all gently; for in the very torrent, tempest, and, as I may say, whirlwind of your passion, you must acquire and beget a temperance that may give it smoothness. O, it offends me to the soul to hear a robustious periwig-pated fellow tear a passion to tatters, to very rags, to split the ears of the groundlings, who, for the most part, are capable of nothing but inexplicable dumb shows and noise. I would have such a fellow whipp'd for o'erdoing Termagant; it out-herods Herod. Pray you avoid it.

Be not too tame neither, but let your own discretion be your tutor. Suit the action to the word, the word to the action; with this special observance, that you o'erstep not the modesty of nature; for anything so o'erdone is from the purpose of playing, whose end, both at the first and now, was and is to hold, as 'twere, the mirror up to nature; to show virtue her own feature, scorn her own image, and the very age and body of the time his form and pressure.

Hamlet

1 Words

> POLONIUS What do you read, my lord?
> HAMLET Words, words, words.

Speech is a method of communicating. There are other ways: one is the body language of GESTURE AND MOVEMENT, which we have already considered; another is the written word – which is where the actor must begin.

Every occupation, science or art evolves its own vocabulary. Shepherds working in remote hillsides have a language to describe their work. Nuclear engineers and computer technicians use another vocabulary. A great dancer is said to have invented a new language of movement. In the theatre we speak of **heightened language**: the use of unusual words to describe unusual experience.

When we are emotionally roused we feel the need for words different and more emphatic than those in daily use. We all feel at times a need to shout and rage. Here is Hamlet doing it:

> Bloody, bawdy villain!
> Remorseless, treacherous, lecherous, kindless villain!
> O, vengeance!   II ii 575-7

Then he realises what he is doing:

> Why, what an ass am I! This is most brave,
> That I, the son of a dear father murder'd,
> Prompted to my revenge by heaven and hell,
> Must, like a whore, unpack my heart with words,
> And fall a-cursing like a very drab,
> A scullion!   II ii 578-83

Here is that poor little Doll Tearsheet, in *Henry IV Part Two,* expressing her feelings:

> Away, you cut-purse rascal! you filthy bung, away! By this wine, I'll thrust my knife in your mouldy chaps, an you play the saucy cuttle with me. Away, you bottle-ale rascal! you basket-hilt stale juggler, you! Since when, I pray you, sir? God's light, with two points on your shoulder? Much!... Captain! Thou abominable damn'd cheater, art thou not ashamed to be called captain? An captains were of my mind, they would truncheon you out, for taking their names upon you before you have earn'd them. You a captain! you slave, for what? For tearing a poor whore's ruff in a bawdy-house? He a captain! hang him, rogue! He lives upon mouldy stew'd prunes and dried cakes. A captain! God's light, these villains will make the word as odious as the word 'occupy';

which was an excellent good word before it was ill sorted. Therefore
captains had need look to't.   II iv 120-141

In both passages there is a wonderful use of words. Hamlet expresses his anger,
then his disgust with himself for doing it in that way. In Doll's harangue there are
several words no longer in common use but if you care to look them up in a glossary, or a dictionary of old words, you will find they were fairly precise as she used
them, and at the end there is her dissatisfaction that the word 'occupy' has been
spoilt with misuse. And in the middle, there is a phrase that tells us of Pistol's
coarseness and brutality and her vulnerability: 'tear a poor whore's ruff' – her one
piece of probably shabby but treasured finery. In the midst of all her vituperation,
that phrase can bring a lump to the throat. We learn so much about her life.

Characters using 'bad language', of which we are sometimes forewarned in a
title or programme note, appear in many present-day plays. As always, this kind
of dialogue depends on the skill of the playwright if it is not to become boring. In
the plays of David Mamet, it attains a kind of crazy poetry. But it needs careful
handling on the part of the actor. It is all too easy to heighten energy and vocal
level, to generalise and become tedious. On the stage the actor must be in total
control of himself. His traffic is words.

We think in words. Feeling becomes thought; the words we use are the shape
of that thought. We are pleased when we can describe accurately what we feel,
and frustrated when we fail to explain ourselves. We use what are called swear-
words to give force to our meaning.

The original meaning of many of these words has long been left behind. For
example, how many people using the word 'bloody' realise that it means 'by our
Lady'? To use it in the wrong context was an insult to the Virgin Mary and
therefore sinful. Swear-words are for the most part corruptions of the words or
phrases that were used when taking oaths. They were quite literally 'swear' words.
Oaths and curses were once a vital part of the language, not just in Shakespeare's
time but for hundreds of years before. To break a sworn oath was a serious matter
and the more sacred the words used in taking the oath, the greater the sin in
breaking it. A curse could have a terrible effect: the power of the curse to cause
harm was a deeply-held belief, and the recipient of the curse was often deeply
disturbed and depressed by it. We can still feel like that at times. Someone accuses us of having done something monstrous. It may be totally untrue, or it may be
based on total misapprehension. None the less, we are worried and unhappy. The
power of words!

The custom of calling down curses – as the characters do in Shakespeare's
History Plays or in *King Lear* – is no longer with us, but it is as well to consider
the effect they had at the time. The curse that Lady Anne wishes on Richard,
over the butchered body of her father-in-law, is horrible:

Curs'd be the hand that made these fatal holes!
Cursed the heart that had the heart to do it!

Cursed the blood that let this blood from hence!
More direful hap betide that hated wretch
That makes us wretched by the death of thee
Than I can wish to adders, spiders, toads,
Or any creeping venom'd thing that lives!   I ii 14-20

But probably the worst and most terrifyingly-worded is Lear's curse on Goneril:

Hear, Nature, hear; dear goddess, hear.
Suspend thy purpose, if thou didst intend
To make this creature fruitful.
Into her womb convey sterility;
Dry up in her the organs of increase;
And from her derogate body never spring
A babe to honour her! If she must teem,
Create her child of spleen, that it may live
And be a thwart disnatur'd torment to her.
Let it stamp wrinkles in her brow of youth,
With cadent tears fret channels in her cheeks,
Turn all her mother's pains and benefits
To laughter and contempt, that she may feel
How sharper than a serpent's tooth it is
To have a thankless child.   I iv 275-289

Not only were curses dreaded and felt to be frightening, but great attention was given to prophecies. There is a strange contradiction of beliefs in the sixteenth century (but probably no stranger than our mish-mash of beliefs today): people believed in the literal truth of the Bible and the prophecies it contained; at the same time they believed in the influence of the stars on their daily lives. Such states of mind are evoked to marvellous effect in *Macbeth*. In that play, the idea of prophecies and the danger of trusting to them is used ironically, capturing the ambiguity inherent in all fortune-telling and prophecy. The predictions made by the witches do indeed come true, but not in the way expected by Macbeth.

The clear, rhythmical style of Bernard Shaw and Granville Barker was a natural inheritance from the writers of the nineteenth century and earlier, steeped in a writing style much influenced by the clarity, power and grace of the King James Bible. It was read aloud in church and school and home. The translation was commissioned by James I in the early seventeenth century, and has been the one most commonly used from his day to ours – almost four hundred years. The work of a group of men whose names we do not know, it set the standard for the writers who came after them, because of their superb use of the English language – the balance of their sentences and the wonderful imagery, the simplicity and music of their cadences.

Shakespeare and his contemporaries were of the generation who made that great translation of the Bible. They used language with a similar freshness and power. For inspiration, they drew on the great myths and legends of Greece and the history of the Roman world: censorship in this period prevented any direct reference to contemporary politics or religious dogma – these were areas where feeling was so strong that men were dying for what they believed – but dramatists could and did use the stories and myths of the past as parables for the present. The way the words were used had often to be ambiguous; the hidden significance of what was being said enriched the written text – this was especially true of dramatic text which would be played out before a sophisticated audience alive to its nuances.

Shakespeare also drew on what he knew and experienced of the life which surrounded him at Stratford and in London. So we have, in *A Midsummer Night's Dream*, 'Duke' Theseus – though there were no dukes in ancient Greece; it's really a portrait of an English country squire, educated, witty, with an acute understanding of the people around him. Shakespeare has given Theseus a speech that contains the perfect description of a poet's mind:

> The poet's eye, in a fine frenzy rolling,
> Doth glance from heaven to earth, from earth to heaven;
> And as imagination bodies forth
> The forms of things unknown, the poet's pen
> Turns them to shapes, and gives to airy nothing
> A local habitation and a name.   V i 12-17

The figure of Theseus belongs to mythology, but Shakespeare's Romans belong to history. Shakespeare evidently had a copy of Sir Thomas North's translation of Plutarch's *Lives of the Noble Grecians and Romans*. The book must have been held together with whatever was the Elizabethan version of sellotape by the time he came to write *Antony and Cleopatra*. In the *Dream* he is creating characters from his own imagination, prompted by his reading, but in *Antony and Cleopatra*, Enobarbus' famous description of Cleopatra is Plutarch's factual prose transformed into exquisite poetry.

> The barge she sat in, like a burnish'd throne,
> Burn'd on the water. The poop was beaten gold;
> Purple the sails, and so perfumed that
> The winds were love-sick with them; the oars were silver,
> Which to the tune of flutes kept stroke, and made
> The water which they beat to follow faster,
> As amorous of their strokes. For her own person,
> It beggar'd all description. She did lie
> In her pavilion, cloth-of-gold, of tissue,
> O'erpicturing that Venus where we see
> The fancy out-work nature. On each side her

Stood pretty dimpled boys, like smiling Cupids,
With divers-colour'd fans, whose wind did seem
To glow the delicate cheeks which they did cool,
And what they undid did.   II ii 195-209

Words, words, words – but such words!

2 Prose

I am frequently surprised when students ask me, 'What is prose?'

In Moliere's famous play *Le Bourgeois Gentilhomme*, a newly rich merchant wants to become a gentleman, to move up in society. He hires tutors for himself – a fencing master, a dancing master and so on – and, of course, someone to teach him to speak correctly. To his great delight he discovers that he has been speaking prose. He takes this to be a sign of intellectual superiority, not realising that prose is all that we use in everyday speech.

This is the kind of definition you will find in the dictionary:

prose, *n.* ordinary non-metrical form of written and spoken language.

I am writing prose at this moment. The significant units are the sentence, paragraph and chapter; pauses and changes of thought are marked by punctuation, not marked by line endings as is the case with VERSE AND POETRY which can be instantly recognised by its shape on the page. Verse is a metrical form of language whose significant units are measured in feet, lines, stanzas and so on. It is written out line by line, even when the sense sometimes runs over into the next line. Verse has a regular beat running through it. Prose does not.

Bernard Shaw, who had at one time been a music critic and was always deeply interested in acting and the training of actors, used to tell students, 'A full stop is four beats, a colon three beats, a semi-colon two, and a comma one.' This is splendid advice if you remember that in music the time-signature gives you the beat and the composer indicates the overall speed by writing a word, such as *lento* or *presto*, at the beginning of a piece. Just as in music a rest denotes a pause, so does a punctuation mark in speech. Some pauses are longer than others, but the music continues through the silence – the feeling continues – as it should with acting.

Here is a speech from Shaw's play *Heartbreak House* (Act II):

MAZZINI DUNN No: I'm no good at making money. I don't care enough for it, somehow. I'm not ambitious! that must be it. Mangan is wonderful about money he thinks of nothing else. He is so dreadfully afraid of being poor. I am always thinking of other things: even at the works I think of the things we are doing and not of what they cost.

And the worst of it is, poor Mangan doesn't know what to do with his money when he gets it. He is such a baby that he doesn't even know what to eat and drink: he has ruined his liver eating and drinking the wrong things; and now he can hardly eat at all. Ellie will diet him splendidly. You will be surprised when you come to know him better: he is really the most helpless of mortals. You get quite a protective feeling towards him.

A **full stop** marks a halt in the procession of thought. It is followed by an entirely new thought – though of course, the new thought may be about the same subject.

A **colon** marks a slightly shorter pause; the phrase that follows is not an entirely new thought, but a variation of the one just spoken.

A **semi-colon** makes a pause which is slightly longer than that marked by a comma.

A **comma** suggests only a very slight pause.

The speech above begins with a strong first syllable followed by a colon. You will probably find that after saying, 'No' you take a very slight breath before continuing to the end of the sentence. Having completed the statement about yourself, a new thought occurs to you. If you make a count of four to yourself through the speech you will find that you have just the right amount of time to get to that thought. Is it a new thought or an addition to the one just spoken?

Here is a piece of dialogue from the third act of the same play:

SHOTOVER At sea nothing happens to the sea. Nothing happens to the sky. The sun comes up from the east and goes down to the west. The moon grows from a sickle to an arc lamp, and comes later and later until she is lost in the light as other things are lost in the darkness. After the typhoon, the flying-fish glitter in the sunshine like birds. It's amazing how they get along, all things considered. Nothing happens, except something not worth mentioning.

ELLIE What is that, O Captain, my captain?

SHOTOVER Nothing but the smash of the drunken skipper's ship on the rocks, the splintering of her rotten timbers, the tearing of her rusty plates, the drowning of the crew like rats in a trap.

ELLIE Moral: don't take rum.

SHOTOVER That is a lie, child. Let a man drink ten barrels of rum a day, he is not a drunken skipper until he is a drifting skipper. Whilst he can lay his course and stand on the bridge and steer it, he is no drunkard. It is the man who lies drinking in his bunk and trusts to Providence that I call the drunken skipper, though he drank nothing but the waters of the River Jordan.

Shaw directs the actor playing Captain Shotover to speak the second section 'savagely' and the third 'vehemently'. I have omitted these directions because they can be misleading for an inexperienced actor, encouraging him to go for feeling before he has explored the content. Go over the speech quietly first. When you feel that you know what is in Shotover's mind, then try Shaw's suggestions.

Now a speech from the work of Harold Pinter – *No Man's Land*. Like the first passage from *Heartbreak House* it is a man explaining himself. Once again, see how punctuation indicates a change of thought; notice how important it is to finish one thought before you start another. But see how the thought just spoken suggests the next and how frequently the line builds to the last word. Try it out, taking just as much time as you need to finish one thought and start the next.

May I say how very kind it was of you to ask me in? In fact, you are kindness itself, probably always are kindness itself, now and in England and in Hampstead and for all eternity.

(He looks about the room.)

What a remarkably pleasant room. I feel at peace here. Safe from all danger. But please don't be alarmed. I shan't stay long. I never stay long, with others. They do not wish it. And that, for me, is a happy state of affairs. My only security, you see, my true comfort and solace, rests in the confirmation that I elicit from people of all kinds a common and constant level of indifference. It assures me that I am as I think myself to be, that I am fixed, concrete. To show interest in me or, good gracious, anything tending towards a positive liking of me, would cause in me a condition of the acutest alarm. Fortunately, the danger is remote.

(Pause)

I speak to you with this startling candour because you are clearly a reticent man, which appeals, and because you are a stranger to me, and because you are clearly kindness itself.

(Pause)

Do you often hang about Hampstead Heath?

Here is a passage from *Gotcha* by another modern playwright, Barrie Keeffe:

KID It's mine. My property. I mean, like the way I gathered… this report here in me pocket, it's what I show the employment exchange,

an' that – to get a job. And all them things you lot… teachers …
written on it. Well, way I see it, none of them didn't exactly like do me
a favour. None of that gonna help me much – specially what *you* wrote.
Headmaster's comment, at the bottom, God's word, the big deal – the
final sentence, end of trial – judge's verdict. (Pause) Achieved little
here… not a success… (Pause) That's what you wrote, an' signed it an'
– (Slight pause) An' now you tell me you don't know who the fuck I
am! […] Farty there? He don't know me from Adam. And her? She
don't know me. An' you don't. I'm the only bleeder here who knows
who I am!

And here is Shakespeare using prose – in *As You Like It*. Rosalind is doing an
efficient debunking job on extravagant romanticism:

> …The poor world is almost six thousand years old, and in all this time
> there was not any man died in his own person, videlicet, in a love-
> cause. Troilus had his brains dash'd out with a Grecian club; yet he did
> what he could to die before, and he is one of the patterns of love.
> Leander, he would have liv'd many a fair year, though Hero had turn'd
> nun, if it had not been for a hot midsummer-night; for, good youth, he
> went but forth to wash him in the Hellespont, and, being taken with
> the cramp, was drown'd; and the foolish chroniclers of that age found
> it was – Hero of Sestos. But these are all lies: men have died from time
> to time, and worms have eaten them, but not for love.   IV i 83ff

Five examples of prose used skilfully to express character. Go over each one
and try out the indicated length of the pauses. Explore also the length of the
pauses between the punctuation marks. Should some phrases be spoken faster
than others because the mind of the speaker is working faster – or slower, as the
case may be? Do not feel restricted by the punctuation. Ask yourself if it really
defines the sense of the passage. Could you yourself in speaking take a longer or a
shorter pause, and if so, why?

3 Grammar

This is a deliberately simple section for those of you who may not have learnt
grammar at school. Some schools no longer teach it, believing that having to
think about the rules of grammar inhibits a child's creativity. The idea is
arguable, but on arriving at drama school and hearing a tutor speak of the
stressing of nouns and main action verbs rather than adjectives and adverbs, it
would be nice to know what he was talking about without having to ask.

You may ask, 'What has grammar to do with acting?' The answer is, nothing directly, but most acting uses words, and words join together and form

patterns, and those patterns we call language, which is our most important means of communication. Language has a structure and that structure we call grammar. A knowledge of grammar and grammatical terms is the most effective way to talk about the structure of a text and to understand how it should sound.

Let us get down to basics. Our prehistoric ancestors having discovered words – sounds that denoted meaning – began to realise that they could be used in more than one way. We began by naming things – our fellow creatures and the objects in the natural world in which we lived, animals, trees, plants. But these things did not stay still. Animals ran and jumped, trees and plants grew. So we had to find words to describe what these things did and when they did them; in the past, in the future or now, in the present. The names of objects – animals, trees – we call **nouns**, and the words that describe things that are done – run, grow – are **verbs**.

There had to be words to describe the objects – were they big or small, beautiful or ugly? What colour were they? These are the words we call **adjectives**. There had to be words to describe how the things were done – fast or slow, well or badly, and so on. The words that describe what the verbs are doing we call **adverbs**.

By arranging all these words in different ways, we found we could change the meaning. We began to structure our language. We made rules so that we should remember the arrangement and be able to create it again. This was how grammar came about

Most of you probably did learn grammar at school. I did, and very boring I found it. All that parsing and analysing – conjunctives and demonstratives and all the rest. Next to arithmetic, it was the most boring subject in the timetable. No one ever said what it was for! However, enough of it stuck and eventually I was very thankful that I had learnt it. Knowing the structure of a text, knowing why it is written the way it is written, is a help to understanding the meaning and knowing how to say it. If you do feel totally ignorant on the subject of grammar, I suggest you get yourself a good grammar textbook. In the meantime, when you are told to stress the nouns or the verbs, you now at least know which words to look for. Stress, by the way, does not mean that you should speak that word louder, but allow it to take the weight of the meaning of the thought or sentence. It is a good rule of thumb not to emphasise the adjectives and adverbs. They are not as important as the nouns and verbs, but are added to them to make a particular meaning clearer.

If you want information about pronouns, prepositions and conjunctions I am afraid you will have to get yourself that good English grammar. (See BOOKS: HISTORY AND GRAMMAR at the end of this book for a recommended work.)

4 Verse and poetry

The first stories you were ever told were probably in verse – nursery rhymes like Little Miss Muffet and Jack and Jill. You may even have been bounced on the knee of some grown-up who recited them as they beat the rhythm.

Stamping, tapping or shouting to a regular beat is enjoyable. When a great number of people do these things in unison it is exciting – think of pop concerts and all-night rave parties. Excitement is a human need. Along with our ancestors' discoveries about the spoken word – indeed, probably before they discovered the spoken word – physical rhythms had become an indispensable part of human culture.

When memorable things happened there was a need to tell others about them, to tell stories. These stories were told in words, sounds and movement, and finally in mimicry. In pretending to be the extraordinary heroes, the gods and goddesses who peopled these stories, acting was born. Since most of these stories were very old, their re-creation owed more to the imagination of those taking part than to historical accuracy. But always these stories were told rhythmically. Poets told them – rhythmically – in verse.

The greatest plays in our theatre were written in Elizabethan and Jacobean times, and many of them were written in verse. Yet verse as a medium in which to write plays was used less and less frequently after the seventeenth century. Or rather, one tends to think that, because the great bulk of plays of the eighteenth and nineteenth centuries which are still widely performed are comedies written in prose. Let us say the more successful plays ceased to be written in verse. From the seventeenth century on, verse became the accepted medium for tragedy, and prose for comedy. It was an unfortunate division. Tragedy, it was felt, must be magnificent and all the characters noble, and the right style in which to write a kind of speech which was thought suitable for people to speak in plays of this time was verse. Sadly, many of these playwrights, through a great admiration for Shakespeare, copied what they thought he had done without really understanding what made him a great dramatist, so although some of these plays are still known to us, most are tediously pretentious. Fortunately for us, the great majority of writers of the period preferred to write comedy. Instead of thinking up improbable events in which to involve kings and princes who bore no resemblance whatsoever to those living and reigning at the time, the comedy writers looked at people in the world around them and described their sometimes outrageous behaviour in the simple hearty prose which could be heard in the streets and coffee houses that surrounded the theatres.

Why did verse cease to be the most important way of writing plays? When did it become ousted by prose? Well, let us look in detail at how plays first came to be written in verse

Michael Alexander, translator of the *Beowulf* in the Penguin edition, reminds us in his introduction to this Old English poem that the poetry was usually chanted aloud or sung and that *Beowulf* was written to be performed. For full appreciation, it should be read aloud. This is what we have to remember about the text of a play – it is written to be listened to, not read.

Beowulf was written many years before our first surviving play text, but it is intriguing to look at a short passage. Try reading it aloud.

> It speaks for itself, my son of Edgelaf,
> that Grendel had never grown such a terror,
> this demon had never dealt your lord
> such havoc in Heorot, had your heart's intention
> been so grim for battle as you give us to believe.
> He's learnt there's in fact not the least need
> excessively to respect the spite of this people,
> the scathing steel-thresh of the Scylding nation.
> He spares not a single sprig of your Danes
> in extorting his tribute, but treats himself proud,
> butchering and dispatching, and expects no resistance
> from the spear-wielding Scyldings.   591-602

Now here is a passage from the York Mystery Cycle, the opening of *The Play of Creation*. It is more difficult than the *Beowulf* because it has been adapted, not translated, and the adapter has kept many words which are not now in use. He has quite rightly wanted to change as little as possible of the original. But it works wonderfully when spoken. Again, read it aloud to yourself:

> I am gracious and great, God without beginning;
> I am maker unmade, all might is in me;
> I am life and the way unto all wealth winning;
> I am foremost and first, as I bid it shall be.
> On blessing my blee shall be bending,
> And hielding from harm to be binding
> My body in bliss ay abiding,
> Unending without any ending.

Here is another example, this time from *The Play of the Shepherds*, one of the Wakefield Mysteries:

> Lord, what these weathers are cold!
> And I am ill happed.
> I am near-hand dold, so long have I napped;
> My legs they fold, my fingers are chapped.
> It is not as I would, for I am all lapped
> In sorrow.
> In storms and tempest,
> Now in the east, now in the west,

Woe is him that never has rest
Midday or morrow.

And the shepherd goes on grumbling for several more verses about the wretched conditions of his life and how the farmers cheat him out of his rightful earnings. The words are those of everyday speech, but the verse is skilfully structured. Read the piece out loud and you will find that the rhythms are right for the speaker and his situation.

When we come to the language of Shakespeare we encounter something infinitely more complex than anything we have encountered before. Although the examples from *Beowulf* and the mystery plays are not only verse but poetry, we have to realise that not all verse is poetry. Go back for a moment to the nursery rhymes:

Jack and Jill went up the hill
To fetch a pail of water.
Jack fell down and broke his crown
And Jill came tumbling after.

Four short statements; a neat little verse, but is is **poetry**? We should understand that poetry is a word which can be used to describe a feeling about almost any work of art, painting, music or architecture that transcends the ordinary. In a book by L A G Strong, *English For Pleasure*, the author demonstrates the difference between verse and poetry by setting that simple nursery rhyme alongside the following verse, which is also in most collections of nursery rhymes:

How many miles to Babylon?
Fourscore and ten.
Can I get there by candlelight?
Yes, and back again.

What does this do that Jack and Jill does not? Questions and answers are simple and precise, but what is evoked is something mysterious and wonderful.

The name of the city alone stirs the imagination: Babylon, the fabulous city of nearly two thousand years B.C. Think of some of the phrases associated with it. The hanging gardens of Babylon. By the rivers of Babylon we sat down and wept. Babylon, that great city, is fallen.

Is it a child who is asking the questions? Why does he want to go by candlelight? Is it a grown-up replying? A vague answer does not satisfy a child. Babylon is a long way away. By candlelight the child goes to bed. He can go to Babylon in his dreams. Or is it a magic journey we all want to make? There are two more lines:

If you are nimble and light
You may get there by candlelight.

Is it, perhaps, the journey of a creative artist?

5 Shakespeare

There is a problem confronting the director or tutor working with a beginners'
group on a Shakespeare text. What the students already know varies so much.
Some students have studied *Hamlet* or *Othello* for A-level, others have studied a
few of the plays at university. Some will tell you they have worked from the First
Folio; some have played major parts in the plays; some say, quite frankly, that
they hate Shakespeare because they 'did him at school'. A few pretend he is not
all that important and will tell you with a kind of nervous defiance that they do
not know anything at all about Shakespeare and, what is more, they do not want
to know – thereby trying to hold their end up with the well-educated intellectu-
als in the group. Then there are the naturals who have a marvellous ear for verse
– just as some people have a wonderful ear for music – those for whom poetry
matters.

What does one do when faced with such a group? First of all, one has to get
rid of the idea that Shakespeare has to be played in a particular style: certain students have strange and, oddly enough, old-fashioned ideas of how Shakespeare
should be played, and it is the students who encounter Shakespeare's text
absolutely for the first time that may in fact have the advantage. They can find it
difficult at first to read and digest the plays, but as they begin to enjoy them,
their work very often has a delightful freshness and spontaneity.

Very little is known about Shakespeare's early life, but it is known that he was
born in 1564 and lived, until adolescence at least, in the country town of his
birth, Stratford-upon-Avon. In Hamlet's speech to the Players, quoted at the
beginning of this part of the book, Shakespeare speaks of an actor who 'out-
herods Herod' – meaning that he overacts. This is undoubtedly a reference to the
nativity mystery plays well-known at the time, and it is possible that he got his
early experiences of theatre – and perhaps of some overblown performances – by
watching the mystery plays when he was a boy: the nearby city of Coventry was
famed for its cycle of plays.

He was certainly not a university man. The plays he wrote were not intended
as dusty classics – to be studied by generations of wretched essay-writing students. He was an actor writing for actors. His professional life was spent working
with a small group of actors. The principal actor was Richard Burbage, for whom
four of the greatest parts in the history of our theatre were written – Hamlet,
Macbeth, Othello and King Lear – not to mention Berowne, Benedick, Brutus
and Coriolanus.

If I had my way, Shakespeare would not be studied at school except for pleasure: no more essays and paraphrasing and reading what this scholar and that said
about the differences between his early style and his late style. Act him. Talk
about him. Have dictionaries and reference books available so that you can look
up passages that seem obscure because words change their meaning over time.
Look at pictures that show the clothes people wore. Find out what the difficult
religious and political situations were, the subjects that could not be discussed in

the theatre, and above all, what the the audience of the time wanted when they came to the theatre.

Who were those people who filled the Globe on Bankside? Everyone. Everyone from the highest to the lowest. From the nobility sitting on the side of the stage and in the boxes, to the groundlings who stood for three hours to watch the play. The dramatist had to give them what they wanted, otherwise they would not come. Shakespeare and his company were professionals, making a living from the theatre. And they were certainly successful. Shakespeare's renown as a playwright can be dated from his late twenties. Robert Greene, one of the most famous playwrights of the time, warned his fellow writers of this 'upstart crow, beautified with our feathers... he supposes that he is as much able to bombast out a blank verse as the best of you.' By his mid-thirties some were calling Shakespeare the greatest of English dramatists. The dozen or so plays which he had already written, and his company had performed, were so popular that some bookshops were trading in pirated and stolen editions.

They gave the public what the public wanted and what it still wants – entertainment. This is a word which nowadays has unfortunate connotations: the 'entertainment industry' suggests something manufactured to formula, not serious. And of course, not all were capable of being intelligently excited by what they were seeing. In that same speech of Hamlet to the Players, he says of the groundlings that 'for the most part' they were 'capable of nothing but inexplicable dumb shows and noise'. Well, for those there was bear-baiting and quite a few public executions: the most entertaining were probably those where the criminal was hung, drawn and quartered; the Elizabethan period was one of filth and horror as well as poetry, beauty, music and intellectual brilliance. But what Shakespeare and his fellow actors realised was that the public wanted to be continually surprised, made to laugh and cry, to wonder, to argue, to understand themselves by empathising with the characters they watched.

6 Blank verse

The Mystery plays were largely written in rhymed verse with irregular metre. It might be called doggerel. This had long been the accepted form for dramatic writing. But by the time Shakespeare and his contemporaries – Marlowe, Ben Jonson, Beaumont and Fletcher – started to write, a newer dramatic form had just been introduced into England from Italy, and was becoming widely used.

A general definition for blank verse would be 'unrhymed verse', but the form which was popular in Shakespeare's day was more specifically unrhymed **iambic pentameter**. (What this is we will deal with in a moment.) Shakespeare wrote much of his verse in iambic pentameter, and whether or not he believed as a young writer that he could 'bombast out a blank verse', it is clear that he developed the form to perfection. But Shakespeare's texts are by no means all iambic pentameter. We have already seen that he wrote very effectively in prose; he also used other verse forms, rhymed and unrhymed, and he used other metres.

Before we are able to understand what iambic pentameter is, we need to know about **metre**. I have tried to work out some simple but accurate definitions. I have gone through dictionaries and books of reference. It has often seemed that the explanations were so difficult that I should have to explain the explanations! Let us start with two words that can cause confusion, meter and metre. Both mean measure, but the first is used for a machine into which you insert coins when you want to park your car, or pay for electricity; the second is a measure of verse. (Although, just to confuse you, the spelling changes when used in a word like pentameter – which means five metres.)

What does metre measure? The length of a line of verse and its rhythm. In verse, each unit of measurement is called a **foot**. Every line of verse contains a number of feet – that is, a succession of one or more syllables. The foot is something like a time-signature in music which tells you how many notes in a bar and its rhythm. So just as there is waltz-time and march-time, there are different types of foot. The **trochee**, for example, is a stressed, or long, syllable, followed by an unstressed, or short syllable. It is pronounced TRO-key, with the stress on the first syllable. If you think about it you will see that the word 'trochee' is itself a trochee. The **iamb** is precisely the opposite – unstressed followed by stressed – and, yes, the word 'iamb' is also an example of an iambic foot.

The poet Samuel Coleridge wrote this useful little verse to help his son remember the different metres:

> Trochee trips from long to short:
> From long to long in solemn sort
> Slow Spondee stalks; strong foot! yet ill able
> Ever to come up with Dactyl trisyllable
> Iambics march from short to long;
> With a leap and a bound the swift Anapaests throng.

The length of a line is expressed by the number of feet it contains. Monometer, dimeter, trimeter, tetrameter, pentameter, hexameter, are named according to the number of feet in their composition. The first line of the above poem would be termed trochaic tetrameter because it contains four trochees.

You are now in a position to deduce what iambic pentameter is!

While a singer has bars marked out with lines and time-signatures, the actor has to work out the rhythm of the verse for himself. I say work it out because we are not all born with an ear for verse any more than we are with a musical ear. But most of us can hear the differences and, as we begin to appreciate them, so our ear becomes attuned to the rightness of a line.

Here is an early example of dramatic blank verse from *Gorboduc* by Thomas Norton and Thomas Sackville, the first English tragedy to be written in iambic

pentameter, a quarter of a century before Marlowe, Shakespeare, Ben Jonson and
the others began to develop the form:

> O king, the greatest grief that ever prince did hear,
> That ever woeful messenger did tell,
> That ever wretched land had seen before,
> I bring to you: Porrex, your younger son,
> With sudden force invaded hath the land
> That you Ferrex did allot to rule,
> And with his own most bloody hand he hath
> His brother slain and doth possess the real.

To which the king replies:

> O heavens, send down the flames of your revenge!
> Destroy, I say, with flash of wreakful fire
> The traitor son and then the wretched sire!
> But let us go, that yet perhaps I may
> Die with revenge, and pease the hateful gods.

You can beat out the iambic there. It sounds repetitive and dull. But do not
let us be too derogatory. In its day it was a great play. It had something to say
about the division of a kingdom – which was of concern to the audience of the
time – and the rhythm in which it was spoken probably seemed as fresh and
interesting as the rhythms of Beckett and Pinter to later generations. This did
not, of course, stop the immediate successors of Sackville and Norton improving
on what had been done.

In its earliest form, each line of blank verse tended to be a self-contained
thought. It was **end-stopped**. The sense seldom ran over into the next line and
most lines ended with a punctuation mark, either a comma, a semi-colon or a full
stop. Iambic pentameter could accurately capture the rhythm of natural speech,
but the cumulative effect of end-stopping was monotonous regularity. It needed
to be made more flexible as a vehicle for dramatic expression. As he developed as
a writer, Shakespeare found ways of 'naturalising' blank verse. Let us take a well-
known speech from *Julius Caesar* that is almost all end-stopped:

> Friends, Romans, countrymen, lend me your ears;
> I come to bury Caesar, not to praise him.
> The evil that men do lives after them;
> The good is oft interred with their bones;
> So let it be with Caesar.   III ii 73-77

And so on right through the speech. Antony has to win over a mob who
seem already to be strongly siding with Brutus. The strong statements and the

pauses at the end of each line give time for the reverberation of sound to die away and also give what he has to say force and time to sink in.

To get around the rigidity of the end-stopping, Shakespeare made use of the **overflow** line, where the sense runs over into the next. The lines are made to serve the sentences and not the other way round. A run-over line has been likened to a diving board. You pace up the line and then take a spring up and into the next. I find it a very helpful image, conjuring up the suspense and excitement while the diver is in the air. Try it out for yourself with the following passage, also from *Julius Caesar*, which combines end-stopped lines with lines that overflow:

> No, not an oath. If not the face of men,
> The sufferance of our souls, the time's abuse,
> If these be motives weak, break off betimes,
> And every man hence to his idle bed.
> So let high-sighted tyranny range on,
> Till each man drop by lottery. But if these,
> As I am sure they do, bear fire enough
> To kindle cowards, and to steel with valour
> The melting spirits of women, then, countrymen,
> What need we any spur but our own cause
> To prick us to redress? What other bond
> Than secret Romans that have spoke the word
> And will not palter? And what other oath
> Than honesty to honesty engag'd
> That this shall be or we will fall for it?   II i 114-128

The continuation of the sense from one line to another is sometimes spoken of as **enjambement** (from the French word *enjamber* – to stride over). A **suspensory pause**, on the other hand, is the pause of suspense at the end of a run-over line, before the thought is finally completed with the next line or lines. Suspense is the essence of drama, of dramatic story-telling. With Jack and Jill you pause at the end of each line because you want to make sure that the child has got the idea, that he is ready for the next one; you dramatise your story, hold back the action, to make it more exciting. But too often actors pause because they are demonstrating thinking. They pause before a word in order to show the audience that they are intelligent, thinking actors. But they are not thinking, they are merely thinking about thinking; it is just a boring trick. Anyway, none of Shakespeare's characters is ever at a loss for a word. They may not always get the word right – Dogberry and Bottom do not – but they never hesitate; they are highly articulate.

The **caesura** is a mid-line pause when the thought has reached its conclusion. If the poet were to continue the thought of a run-over line to the end of the next line, and if the pattern were sustained – if, say, every other line were end-stopped – the versification would again become monotonous. But if a stop is made at some point in the line before the thought reaches its climax and the actor has held the pause for as long as he finds truthful, then we are eager to go on with him.

Pauses can be wonderful or they can be deadly. The important thing to remember is that a pause is not a stop. It is like a rest in music. The music goes on through the silence. The feeling goes on through the pause. Do not let the feeling die away at the end of the line. End-stopped or overflowed, the feeling at the end of the line is stronger than it was at the beginning. The line builds to the last word. Look at the final words of some of the lines from the passage just quoted and see how strong they are and how they reverberate. Too often actors make the beginning of the line stronger than the end, but if you do that with the speech, see how it weakens it. Take the line:

Than secret Romans that have spoke the word

All too often the actor will stress 'secret' and then let the line lose energy until the last word is barely audible. Another old bogy is the falling inflection. Students try to cure this when told about it by pitching the last word up. That usually makes nonsense of the line. What has not been understood is that the fall is not in volume, but in energy of thought.

Try Brutus' line again. This time, try to give 'word' an enormous importance. Do not speak it louder, but with much greater intensity. The word of a Roman is something he lives by, it can never be doubted. Having spoken it, look at your hearers. Have they understood? It is something mystical, wonderful, Roman. Look at the other lines and compare the importance of the second half with the first. Do it all the time with every line you speak.

The following passage from *The Winter's Tale* is a good example of lines building to the last word. To help you avoid attacking the first part of the line very strongly and running out of energy on the second half, it is quite a good idea – before starting to memorise – to mark the line where you think the caesura (or mid-line pause) would come. I have marked the passage to denote my selection. If you read the speech phrase by phrase, taking a slight pause where the caesura comes and making your thought stronger in the second half of the line, you will find that your speech rhythms express the speaker's considerable interest in the gentleman she is talking about.

> What studied torments, tyrant, / hast for me?
> What wheels, racks, fires? / What flaying, boiling
> In leads or oils? / What old or newer torture
> Must I receive, whose every word deserves
> To taste of thy most worst? / Thy tyranny
> Together working with thy jealousies,
> Fancies too weak for boys, / too green and idle
> For girls of nine / – O, think what they have done,

And then run mad indeed, / stark mad; / for all
Thy by-gone fooleries were but spices of it.
That thou betray'dst Polixenes, / 'twas nothing;
That did but show thee, of a fool, / inconstant,
And damnable ingrateful. / Nor was't much
Thou wouldst have poison'd good Camillo's honour,
To have him kill a king – / poor trespasses,
More monstrous standing by; / whereof I reckon
The casting forth to crows thy baby daughter
To be or none or little, / though a devil
Would have shed water out of fire ere done't;   III ii 172-190

Along with the mix of end-stopped and overflowing lines, Shakespeare made his blank verse more flexible by breaking up the regularity of the iambic metre. In the above passage you will see that the position of the caesura is not the same in every line but subtly varied. The passage also demonstrates his use of the feminine ending – an unstressed eleventh syllable added to the final stressed tenth. Out of nineteen lines, almost half have eleven syllables, the final one unstressed, but when you come to speak them you will find the extra syllable creates a reverberation that helps sustain the vigour of the thought. Most of the lines overflow. The main pauses are at the mid-line, but there is a strong emphasis on the end of each line. The complex rhythms that result are those of a woman beside herself with indignation.

7 Speaking the speech

I have gone into blank verse in some detail because students will sometimes try to scan the lines for what they understand as a regular iambic beat, believing that this is the clue to speaking Shakespearian verse. Of course, it is confusing because many of the lines can be quite regular, especially in the early plays.

Iambic pentameter was for Shakespeare the verse form nearest to the ordinary speech of the people around him, of the people in the streets, of those aristocrats whom he had heard talking when the company had played in their houses, the way that he himself spoke. We still use the rhythms. Many phrases that we use every day have the iambic beat. British students, especially those who have a good ear, fall naturally into Shakespeare's rhythms but Americans and other students (whose everyday speech includes rhythms from many languages far more recently imported than the Norman-French of William the Conqueror and his followers) do not discover the right stressing so easily. This is why some come to England to train. Then there are other students who believe that if you just go for the feeling everything will be all right. Unfortunately, it will not. Without an understanding of the structure of the verse, which means being able to make the right pauses, and stress the right words, you will not get at the true meaning. You will merely turn good verse into indifferent prose.Here is an example, from *Love's Labour's Lost*, spoken by Rosaline, where every line is defined as iambic.

The variation is achieved in the stressing:

> Another of these students at that time
> Was there with him, / if I have heard a truth.
> Berowne they call him; / but a merrier man,
> Within the limit of becoming mirth,
> I never spent an hour's talk withal.
> His eye / begets occasion for his wit,
> For every object / that the one doth catch
> The other / turns to a mirth-moving jest,
> Which his fair tongue, / conceit's expositor,
> Delivers in such apt and gracious words
> That aged ears / play truant at his tales,
> And younger hearings / are quite ravished;
> So sweet and voluble / is his discourse.   II i 64-76

There are two lines, nine and thirteen, which are not regular if we pronounce them as we would now. The final syllable of 'expositor' was probably stressed in Shakespeare's time. In line eleven, the final 'ed' has to be stressed or the line does not scan. Knowing when and when not to pronounce the final 'ed' can sometimes be a problem if you have an old edition of *The Complete Works of William Shakespeare*. In recent editions of the plays, there is usually an indication as to whether or not to pronounce it. In the text quoted here it is quite simple. If it is pronounced it is written completely (eg. ravished). If it is not pronounced, an apostrophe replaces the 'e' (ravish'd). Some editions such as the Penguin and the Cygnet print an accent over the pronounced syllable (ravishéd).

Coleridge says in his little verse, 'Iambics march from short to long.' Greek prosody, from which these terms are borrowed, is based on quantity (the length of the syllables) and a trochee is, strictly speaking, a long syllable followed by a short one half its length. An iamb (or iambus) is the reverse of this. In English verse however, though quantity plays an important part, stress is the dominating factor.

Let us have a closer look at the iambic metre as it is used by Shakespeare. In order to add further variety to his blank verse he sometimes strayed away from strict iambic pentameter. Technically, you might say he did it by sometimes introducing a trochee, especially in the first foot. But it is often a lot more complicated than that. Look at Titania's famous speech from *A Midsummer Night's Dream* which is done in class and used very frequently for auditions. It begins:

> These are the forgeries of jealousy;
> And never, since the middle summer's spring,
> Met we on hill, in dale, forest, or mead,

> By paved fountain, or by rushy brook,
> Or in the beached margent of the sea,
> To dance our ringlets to the whistling wind,
> But with thy brawls thou hast disturb'd our sport.   II i 81-87

If you try to scan that first line as a regular iambic, all the strong accents come out in the wrong place. But if you take the first foot as a trochee, or reversed iambic foot, then the beginning makes more sense. But then the next strong stress is surely on the first syllable of 'forgeries', and there are two syllables before we get there, and after that there are three short syllables before we get to the first syllable of 'jealousy'. What is Shakespeare doing?

He is doing what poets before him and since have always done. He is hearing his verse musically rather than beating it out academically. He is employing the practice of substitution. He is doing what composers do. When he writes two or three unaccented syllables in place of a single one, he does what the musician does when he writes two or more semi-quavers in place of a quaver.

This means that the actor, in speaking, must be aware of exactly what value he must give these small words – of the lightness, speed and accuracy of the diction he must use – and, although our verse is not, as the Greek, based on duration, we still have to give care and consideration to the duration of vowels. Look at the passage above and think how much it depends for the beauty of its meaning on the sound and arrangement of words. Take the line:

> Or in the beached margent of the sea

This is a regular iambic line with three strong stresses. The first syllable of 'beached', the first syllable of 'margent' and the word 'sea'. If you speak the first three words quite fast and then slow down on 'beached' (here the final syllable of the word is sounded) and 'margent', then lightly over the next two small words to dwell on that final word 'sea', you will find that the line has the sound of a wave coming in, spreading over a beach and coming to stillness. Its effect is known as **onomatopoeia** – using words whose sounds suggest their meaning. The *Dream* is full of such lines. Naturally, the dramatist makes great use of this technique. He is writing his lines to be heard and the actor must use all his skill and subtlety, not only to give them their beauty and meaning, but to make them sound as though they were being spoken for the first time by the character.

There is something else that the actor needs to look for in blank verse. He must observe carefully when the line is short of the full number of syllables and ask himself why. It usually suggests a pause, and the pause should be the length of the missing syllables.

Oberon provokes Titania to the speech we have just been looking at by accusing her of leading Theseus astray. Look at the way he finishes the speech:

> Didst not thou lead him through the glimmering night

From Perigouna, whom he ravished?
And make him with fair Aegles break his faith,
With Ariadne and Antiopa?   II i 77-80

There is a half-line pause before Titania brings her indignation to bear on him with 'These are the forgeries of jealousy.'

See how the names of the ladies are arranged, with the last two as the most resounding – probably the most important. Oberon needs to let those names ring out and Titania needs silence before she lets that first syllable ring out. Then she can build her anger to the end of the line.

Now another piece of text where weak endings are used. It is a speech by Hermione from *The Winter's Tale* which is frequently done in audition:

Since what I am to say must be but that
Which contradicts my accusation, and
The testimony on my part no other
But what comes from myself, it shall scarce boot me
To say 'Not guilty'. / Mine integrity
Being counted falsehood shall, / as I express it,
Be so receiv'd. / But thus – / if pow'rs divine
Behold our human actions, / as they do,
I doubt not then but innocence shall make
False accusation blush, / and tyranny
Tremble at patience.   III ii 20-30

Look at it carefully and you will see that the line endings are quite unlike any of the other pieces quoted. In the first line, there are two syllables at the end of the line which are small, unimportant words – ones that we do not normally emphasise. In the second, there are three; in the third and fourth, one; and in the fifth, two. Then in the seventh line the last syllable is very strong; again in the eighth and ninth; and the final word of the tenth, though it has an unaccented final syllable, ends with a powerful word. Notice all the run-over lines.

Now think of Hermione's situation. She has been imprisoned on a false charge of adultery. In prison, she has borne a child which has immediately been taken from her to be destroyed. She is a queen and the daughter of the Emperor of Russia. She is here in this public place for anyone to see and remark on, and since it is a very short time since the child was born she has not yet recovered her strength. She knows that she has no one to give evidence on her behalf.

When people are very ill or very tired – or, as in this case, both – it is quite difficult to speak at all: breathing is difficult; there are odd pauses. In this speech you will see that the caesuras are, indeed, not where you might expect them.

Take the first line. Most inexperienced actresses make no pause at all at the end of it but go straight on to 'accusation', then make no further pause until they come to 'myself' in the fourth line. Yes, it makes sense, but a brilliant bit of dramatic writing has been turned into nice, neat prose and the actress either treats it accordingly or gives it a dose of emotional acting.

Now try this. Get your imagination going and try to think yourself into a situation where you have been exhausted and miserable, but were trying hard to hold on to your dignity. If you start off and get to the word 'say' you might well feel that you cannot get any further without taking a small breath to finish the line. Even so, you cannot complete the statement, so the word 'that' – which is one we do not usually emphasise – becomes a word that you quite literally have to lean on in order to get enough breath to get to 'accusation'. There you have to pause in order to start again with 'and'. This time you can either get to 'part' or go on to 'other'. Then you go on to 'myself'. And this is marvellous: from now on the pauses seem to get shorter and from the word 'receiv'd', which seems to end the first part of the speech, it is as though the woman is gathering strength. She ends this line with the ringing word 'divine' and the next with a strong assertion 'as they do', and the lines are very strong to the end. What Shakespeare has done is to write the rhythm of the feeling. The verse is an entirely accurate expression of the emotion. You will still have to work hard at the speech to get your feeling and breathing going with it. The dramatist tells you what to do. He does not tell you how you do it!

Begin by using your imagination to understand a text. Then try to find in the skills you have learnt, or are still learning, the best way to express the truth that you feel you have discovered. Do it with a passage from *Cymbeline*, one of the very last of Shakespeare's plays. It is Pisanio who speaks:

> You must forget to be a woman; change
> Command into obedience; fear and niceness –
> The handmaids of all women, or, more truly,
> Woman it pretty self – into a waggish courage;
> Ready in gibes, quick-answer'd, saucy, and
> As quarrelous as the weasel.   III iv 153-158

There you are! Do not bother with the iambic; go for the words that are strongly stressed, the line endings, the mid-line pauses, and a lovely weak ending in the penultimate line. Hold the thought on that final 'and', then you, Pisanio, can venture a joke that, bad as the situation is, will appeal to Imogen's sense of humour. Joy for the actor! What Shakespeare is writing here is free verse!

8 Voice

A great star of the past was once asked what was the actor's most important asset, and replied, 'Voice, voice and yet more voice.' One might qualify that by saying that had he been asked what the actor's most important physical asset was he would have been right, but perhaps he took it for granted that an actor was born with creative imagination, so that the faculty was not worth mentioning.

However, to give the creative imagination full expression – to speak the speech – the actor needs voice.

A beautiful voice is a great asset. It is not a necessity. Several great actors of the past, Kean and Irving among them, were severely criticised for the poor quality of their voices, but no one questioned the way their voices were used.

The dangerous actor should develop a strong voice, one that will not tire, no matter how huge the space and how bad the conditions in which he has to use it, but one which will be sufficiently flexible to enable him to suggest every nuance of feeling in such conditions.

He has to know how his voice works, what its capacity is and how to care for it. This cannot be achieved without good training and hard work, which ideally should continue in daily exercise throughout his whole career. Some actors continue to study with a voice tutor throughout their working life.

Before Olivier started to rehearse *Othello*, he worked with a voice tutor, Barry Smith, to extend the range of his voice. Until then he had seldom needed to use a lower register, but he would need it now. So he worked to extend the range of his voice. Not to change it.

It is not possible to actually change a voice. By hard work, it is possible to increase the range of sound of which it is capable – it was said that Olivier extended his range downwards by an octave – but it is important that such work is supervised by an expert. Working wrongly can ruin a voice. This is why good voice tutors at drama school are severe with students. They have a great responsibility.

It occasionally seems to students that voice tutors watching the acting exercise unduly criticise interpretation, but it not possible to consider the actor's voice without considering what he is being asked to do with it. No matter what the part, however rough the character, whether or not an accent is being used, the actor must produce his voice correctly, and this is not right unless it truthfully expresses the character. Voice tutors study the play and confer with directors. As often as possible they attend rehearsals: a tutor wants to see if the student is putting into practise what has been learnt in class, and then give extra guidance if necessary. This is important. Wrong use of the voice can diminish and even distort an actor's interpretation.

One of the most frequent mistakes made by beginners is the belief that a special voice should be used for acting. Years ago, this idea seems to have prevailed in the professional theatre, and for one reason or another it is still often thought necessary in the amateur world. Students coming from such groups are quite distressed to find that a voice they have been cultivating, and which has been praised, is not their true one, and that they must relearn a whole new way of using the voice. Fortunately, once they are accustomed to the idea they find the new experience more comfortable and artistically satisfying.

The closing pages of Marlowe's *Faustus* make enormous demands on the voice. In his splendid book *The Irresistible Theatre*, W Bridge Adams writes that in the final scene, in which the bond falls due and hell closes in on him, such dexterity and passion is called for in the playing that an actor who is bold enough to attempt it today may soon find himself wondering what he lacks that was possessed by the actors for whom it was written. Like King Lear, Faustus plumbs the depths of human suffering. But he is also a lost soul, and it is with the voice of one already damned – 'scorched and fried in the flames of medieval hell' – that the actor must capture first the pathos of *lente, lente, currite noctis equi* ('O run slowly, slowly, horses of the night'), express the desperate ecstasy of

> O, I'll leap up to my God! Who pulls me down?
> See, see where Christ's blood streams in the firmament!
> One drop would save my soul – half a drop: ah, my Christ!
> Ah, rend not my heart for naming of my Christ!
> Yet will I call on him…

proceed to build through forty lines to reach the pitiless crescendo as the devils enter, and yet keep in reserve some unused notes for his final terrible cry as they drag him away

> Ugly hell, gape not! come not, Lucifer!
> I'll burn my books! – Ah Mephistophilis!

Coquelin, the great French actor of the nineteenth century, once said, 'articulation is to speech what drawing is to painting… the power of a true inflection is incalculable, and all the picturesque exteriors in the world will not move an audience like one cry given with the right intonation. Articulation should therefore be the first study of the actor.'

French actors have one great advantage over English actors; they are not afraid of making noises. Boverio's great cry of 'Ha!' at the end of the first act of *Viol de Lucrece* was unforgettable. With one syllable he filled the theatre with amazement, horror and fear of what was to come. Too often, English actors confronted with 'O' or 'Ha' or 'Fie, fie' will opt out and make nothing of the exclamation, not realising that when a great dramatist indicates a non-verbal sound it is because the feeling has broken the bounds of verbal expression and must explode in pure sound. But the actor will not manage this moment of truth unless lungs, diaphragm and thought are totally and immediately at the command of his creative imagination.

The voice is physical. We create sound by using a physical mechanism in our bodies. We can be taught to use our bodies to maximum effect physically. We cannot be made to use them imaginatively. The possibilities can be opened up to us but that is all that can be done by the most brilliant teacher or director. It is for us to make use of the teaching.

Where does one start with the voice? First of all, observe and listen.

Listen to the way people around you use their voices. How do they use their voice, and for what reason.

Observe the way that you use your own voice. What do you do when you call to someone at a distance? What do you do when you call someone to come and sit by the fire? How do you use it when you are trying to persuade a shy child to come and talk to you? Think how you would use it when hoping to get a timid wild animal to come close.

There are many other such situations that you can invent for yourself. Your voice is uniquely your own. Using these simple methods, you will be making invaluable discoveries about your power and skills as an actor.

In the next part of this book we shall consider some of the techniques you will need to master if you are serious about 'daring to excel'.

blueprint preparing for rehearsal
Lear *King Lear*

What is the actor to take to rehearsal by way of preparation? Something that will enable him to make a definite contribution of his own, but which will not be so rigid that he will find himself in conflict with the director.

Let us suppose that the student is to play the first scene of *King Lear*. This is not as unlikely as it may seem. Directors frequently use a great classical text as material for beginners. There are many reasons for this. It is right that the young actor should know as soon as possible the demands that are likely to be made on him; work on a great text is a splendid way of expanding the imagination; and these texts are so strongly constructed and so imaginatively written that they support the actor. It needs a highly experienced actor to deal with feeble situations and clichéd lines. Furthermore, the great playwrights are marvellously economical: the great scene between Macbeth and Lady Macbeth which ends the second act is only fifty-five lines; the soliloquy which precedes it only twenty-seven; eighty-two lines in which to lay bare a soul and resolve a conflict. One of the greatest scenes in Chekhov's *Three Sisters* is little more than half a page.

The first scene of *King Lear* is 306 lines, introduces no fewer than eight characters – and reveals them clearly for what they really are right at the start of the play. Some are going to change greatly as the play goes on, two not at all and two we shall not see again, but their quality as people central to the unfolding drama is brilliantly disclosed in this opening scene.

Tell a group of young children the story of King Lear and then ask them to play it, and what happens? One of them will start by saying, 'I'm King Lear, you're Kent, you're Goneril' and so on. The others join in, and after a bit of argument they will have the parts allotted and the game begins. Lear enters and tells the rest that he has divided his kingdom and will give the largest share to the one who loves him best. So it goes on. What are these children doing? They are playing the action. From that action they will play the character also. Kent will shout, 'Don't be silly. You're making a mistake.' Lear will shout back. Whether he realises it or not, the child playing Lear has made a basic act of faith. He has said, 'I am King Lear' and he does what Lear does.

If you start by saying, 'I am King Lear', you can then start to ask yourself those two important questions: What do I do? Why do I do it?

Out of these two questions comes everything you need to know about acting. You begin with the basic simplicity of the given actions. The text is like the armature, the internal framework on which a sculptor works. Do not be afraid that this approach will mean oversimplifying. All artists work from something very simple, a basic sketch or design. Gradually they build up the complexities by continually reaching for the answer to the question, 'Why do I do it?'

Let us go through the first scene of *King Lear* asking just those questions.

> My first line is an order to Gloucester. I give an order. I do not make a request. Why? I am a person in authority. I do not ask people to do things for me. I tell them. Quietly perhaps (people who have been in authority all their lives don't bother to raise their voices: they know that they will be obeyed) I give an order. That is my first action.
>
> Next, I tell the waiting court that I am about to reveal a course of action on which I have decided. I demand that a map be handed to me. I then reveal my plan for dividing the kingdom. I explain it carefully and the reasons for it, then ask Goneril to speak.
>
> I listen to what Goneril has to say. Does she say exactly what I expect, or am I amazed and delighted by the warmth of her feeling? Do I, Lear, know what I am going to feel? No. I may know what I expect to feel, but how often is the interview we have imagined like the one that really takes place? No premature decision must be made here, before rehearsal. Wait and see what the actress playing Goneril makes me feel. As the actor, I know what Goneril's future behaviour is going to be – I have read the play. But remember, as the character, I do not.
>
> Whatever my feeling, I do give Goneril her lands – pointing out that they are rich domains – so she must have given me the kind of answer I had been expecting. (Problem here. Why do I give out the prizes before the end of the competition? Perhaps I should put this question to the director.) Next I turn to Regan. I say, 'Dearest Regan…' so it would seem that I am fond of her. Again, I listen to what she says, respond favourably to what the actress makes me feel, and give her lands. Then I turn to Cordelia. 'Now our joy…' It would seem that I have been waiting for this moment.

If Lear means what he says, and his plan to divide the kingdom is a precaution against future strife, then surely giving the largest share to the youngest child is the very thing that will cause it. Can he give Cordelia the largest share without Cornwall or Albany being furious? Only if he can make it appear that she is somehow the most deserving. He does not talk about inheritance, he specifically says 'dower'.

The word 'dower' is used no fewer than six times in the scene and several lines make reference to it. A woman had to have a dower. Among poor people it might be only a goat and one or two pots and pans; but she had to have something. Marriage was a financial arrangement. In the upper classes it was also a political one. Royalty demanded a royal dower. Burgundy makes this perfectly clear.

Surely Goneril and Regan will have had their dower when they married? Possibly not if they married some years ago when Lear was a very active and capable ruler. He would give them something handsome to go on with and the promise of more on his death. But why is he dividing the kingdom now? Well, he probably does feel that he has had enough of the affairs of state (and there is another and more cogent reason we shall find as we dig further into the play) but if Cordelia is to marry someone as important as either France or Burgundy, an enormous dowry will have to be found.

Isn't the competition for his daughters' love rather silly? It would be in a realistic play, but Lear is not a realistic play. It is almost a fairy-tale episode – and competitions of this kind are common enough in myths and fairy tales. But because the actor always likes to feel the ground underneath his feet, it is helpful to see that it has a realistic basis: it is a political trick. Lear could well feel it to be a rather clever and naughty political trick. If all goes as he imagines it will, then Cordelia will get her dowry, and Cornwall and Albany will not be able to complain of unfairness. They will have their wives to blame for not having said the right thing!

For Shakespeare's audience the word 'dower' was loaded with significance. They would probably have understood Lear's dilemma and endorsed what they might have felt to be his astuteness. Can a modern actor make that idea clear to a present-day audience? Probably not without the help of a programme note; but he can know it himself, and that is what is important to the actor. Now let us return to the action.

I, Lear, completely confident of my plan, turn to Cordelia full of hope only to have the whole thing overthrown by a single word.

The shock causes me to repeat that word. Cordelia repeats it. I tell her to think again. I hear what she says now, but do I really take it in? In this passage much will depend on the actress. Once again I tell her to change what she has said. Not only does she not do so but she explains firmly that should she marry, she must give half her love and duty to her husband. She asks the great question, 'Why have my sisters husbands, if they say they love you all?'

She has made it appear not only to my own family, but to all the onlookers in my court, that she loves me less than Goneril or Regan. The plan has collapsed. Rage takes over and I explode: 'Let it be so! Thy truth, then, be thy dower!' (That word again.) I give way to a storm of anger. Why? Is it not what any father does, when, having set up a marvellous future for his favourite child, it is rejected before other people? Old Capulet reacts in the same way. He is deeply hurt and expresses his hurt in rage. The modern father does not use great classical imagery in turning his daughter out of the house. There Lear has the advantage, and so has the actor playing him. He can express exactly the quality and scale of his anger. In real life and in a naturalistic play, the father would probably say, 'Get out of my house. I never want to see you again!'

Kent attempts to interfere, and I round on him. Why? Because he, like Cordelia, is daring to criticise me in front of my family and court. I then let out, probably without meaning to, that it had been my intention to spend the rest of my life with her. Hastily (too hastily?) I improvise a second plan, whereby I divide Cordelia's dowry between Goneril and Regan and live in future with each in turn for one month at a time, insisting only that I retain the title and respect due to a king.

Again Kent speaks up, but I will not hear him. He refuses to be silenced, and this time I hear him out. Why? Perhaps, as an old friend, he may be going to find a way out. But he does not. He reproaches me sternly. Now I am being accused of being swayed by flattery, for being over-hasty and showing a lack of perception. In a fit of fury, I threaten Kent with his life. He still will not be silenced and I banish him. I listen in silence to his farewells. What effect do his words have on me? What effect will they gain from the way that they are spoken? Wait and see what happens in rehearsal.

I maintain silence after he has gone, until Gloucester enters to announce the King of France and Duke of Burgundy. I address myself to Burgundy and ask him what is the least he will take by way of dowry with Cordelia. He replies that he is not asking for more than I would give, but that he does not expect me to offer less. I tell him that Cordelia is now not worth a penny and that I am deeply displeased with her. He merely says he has no answer, so I make my meaning entirely clear. The girl is in disgrace and I am sending her away from me. Burgundy says one cannot choose given such conditions. I am now curt with him. Tell him that he should leave her, and that is that.

I now turn to France, telling him that I consider Cordelia unworthy of his attentions, and suggest that he looks somewhere else for a wife. France (who it would seem has spent his time at Lear's court getting to know Cordelia) wants to know the reason for my change of feeling towards her.

Before I can reply, Cordelia herself speaks and although she asks me to make it clear that she is not in disgrace for any crime or immorality, she leaves France in no doubt as to what has really happened. France, the one sensible and clear-sighted man in the whole assembly, shows a sense of true values. He allows Burgundy to make an offer for Cordelia, presumably giving the girl a chance to make her own choice. But for Burgundy, it is no dowry, no marriage. And I, Lear, repeat, 'Nothing! I have sworn; I am firm.'

Burgundy expresses regret that Cordelia, losing a dowry, must also lose a husband. She replies that if money means so much to him she will certainly not be his wife. France, in a marvellously beautiful speech, makes it clear how highly he values Cordelia. What happens to me while that speech is being spoken? Am I relieved that Cordelia has, after all, found a splendid husband? Do I feel reproved by the love and generosity of France? I have sworn an oath; I cannot go back on it even if I want to, so France must have her. I will not see her again and she can go without my love and blessing. Taking Burgundy with me, I leave.

Now there are a host of questions to be asked about each of those actions.

I have already suggested why Lear might have set up this competition which we, in our time, find difficult to accept as the action of a normal commonsense human being. But Lear is not a normal commonsense human being. He is eighty, and that would suggest that he has been king for a very long time. An absolute monarch, what we would call a dictator, he has come to expect obedience and flattery as a matter of course.

For someone who is so obviously autocratic, it seems that he decides to retire from the active life of a monarch, and I said earlier that he has probably had enough of the affairs of state, but there might be another, more cogent, reason for it. I think what he fears is senility.

There are moments in Act Two when he is not thinking with any great clarity, and there are two very revealing phrases: 'Do not make me mad' and 'O fool, I shall go mad.' His behaviour in the first scene is that of an old man. Old people can be very healthy and very wise, but they are no longer quick. Their reactions have slowed down. Confronted by Cordelia's 'Nothing', Lear cannot adjust to this new and unexpected situation: he finds himself frustrated and does what old people do when they cannot adjust quickly enough – he responds with anger. Before he has time to think or calm down, Kent has made the situation worse. Then follows the recklessly improvised scheme – again something that old people do because they have to show that they are still in control.

For Lear, the situation is a disaster.

technique

The best analysis of a play is to

act it in the given circumstances

Simple physical actions form the firm basis of everything people do in life. Their value to our art lies in the fact that they are organic in any given circumstances

the actor must never forget that the physical actions are

merely an excuse

for evoking inner action

When you have learnt to create this line of action and when your whole attention is directed towards it, we shall be able to guarantee that on coming out onto the stage, you will always do that which is necessary and for the sake of which your art exists

Stanislavski

1 What is technique?

Students sometimes ask this question because they are confused and feel that different tutors give different answers. The tutors are probably saying much the same thing but the student does not always realise it because the wording is not the same.

The Greeks, who are a pretty good authority on things artistic, had a word for it – *technis*. It was the only word they used. So far as they were concerned there was no difference between art and craft. *Technis* meant the thing created and the means used in that creation. They were all one. A great artist was the one with great imagination and the skills to make that vision manifest.

All the skills needed to make manifest the creative vision are physical. The skill needed to imagine the shape of the thing unknown is in the mind. We learn our physical skills from infancy onward. Instinct tells us how to reach to our mother's breast for food and later we learn to grasp a rusk and pull it to our mouth. Later still we are taught a skill for conveying food to our mouths which is less messy than shoving it in by hand. All skills practised over a long period eventually become almost entirely instinctive. Reading, writing, painting, singing, acting – all these skills are physical, but the desire to do them is emotional and mental. A writer, to express himself, must learn to use his pen or typewriter or word processor. In order to be able to express ourselves we have to learn to use tools, and we learn such skills best from those who already have them. So with acting. One must discover the best ways to do it.

The initial discovery of a skill may be difficult. It may seem at times to inhibit the creative instinct. Students become frustrated in the critical sessions which take place after an acting exercise because they are told of their faults in speech and movement. Having to consider these things when acting, they feel, is a hindrance not a help. They feel a lack of freedom.

Well, there is a freedom certainly, when you run about and enjoy yourself, or when you dance in a disco, but that is not communication. In order to communicate your feelings precisely, you have to find a way of doing it. The more complex the idea you have to communicate, the more skill you need to express it. All creative work demands enormous energy and the ability to struggle with difficulties, but the harder the task, the greater the eventual release and feeling of freedom.

Technique is knowing what you want to do and knowing how to do it. The value of the work created depends on the imagination and the integrity of the artist. In acting there is the inner – **imaginative** – technique, which is subjective: the actor tries to discover the character's feelings and thoughts in order to empathise with him; and there is the outer – **objective** – technique: the actor's work with the text must be objective and involves the search to discover how the dramatist has expressed these feelings and why he has used those words and no others.

Near the end of his life, Stanislavski wrote the words that appear on the title page of this part of the book. Reasoning has nothing to do with art. Simple physical actions form the basis of everything people do in life, and they stem from an inner action. You have to learn to create that inner action and direct your whole attention towards it.

So we come back to those two questions which an actor must start by asking when working on a part – what am I doing? and why do I do it? – and to this we must now add a third: how do I do it? It is a question of technique.

In the sections that follow we will look more closely at technique.

2 A few definitions

After a week or two in a drama school you begin to feel that there are technical words and phrases used by staff and senior students which do not seem to mean quite what you thought them to mean, or they are being used differently. Sometimes you feel quite bewildered by the assumption that you know all about it, and interrupting the class to explain that you do not is embarrassing. Well, here – in alphabetical order – are a few brief definitions of some of these words and phrases.

One of the problems of acting is that there is, at present, no language or specific terminology for what we do in rehearsal. Directors will coin phrases for themselves, or use terms of a particular group or method with which they have been associated. Just as the language we use every day is always changing in subtle ways, so the language, jargon or slang that the directors use also changes. American phraseology differs from British. The British, it seems, have a deep-rooted dislike of polysyllabic words.

I was brought up with the precept that one should never use a word of three syllables if there is a word of two, and never use a word of two syllables if there was a word of one, and never use a Latin derivation if there was an Anglo-Saxon word. It has stood me in good stead. The simple Anglo-Saxon words have a great advantage – they do not go out of fashion. So I do not say, 'What is the motivation?' I just ask, as actors did long before I was born, 'Why are you doing it?'

I have always tried to stick to these basic words and simple expressions in my classes. Otherwise I might be using a fashionable phraseology that becomes dated before my students secure their first job. As Lady Markby says in Oscar Wilde's *An Ideal Husband*, 'Nothing is so dangerous as being too modern. One is apt to grow old-fashioned quite suddenly.'

There are words and phrases which seem to have been in use for a good many years and I will try to define those most generally used and which seem to be likely to be in use for a good many more.

Communication and subtext

Examine the dialogue of a play and you will find that it consists of stating a fact or asking a question. You are either giving or asking for information. You state a fact because you want someone to know it. You ask a question because you want to know something. That may seem very stark and unimaginative.

Of course, there are times when you are not just stating a fact but are using words to explain the kind of fact it is, and those words explain the kind of person that you are. Here are some lines from *A Midsummer Night's Dream*. Lysander is speaking to Helena:

> Why should you think that I should woo in scorn?
> Scorn and derision never come in tears.
> Look when I vow, I weep; and vows so born,
> In their nativity all truth appears.
> How can these things in me seem scorn to you,
> Bearing the badge of faith, to prove them true?   III ii 122-27

Line one is a question and line two a fact. Line three differs. Here an order is being given. Helena is told to observe his condition. Then comes information about the quality of his vows. The last two lines are a question, which is made more urgent by the description of his feelings.

Now, subtext. The reason why Lysander is speaking is clear from what he is saying. But there are times when a statement is not so clear-cut, or there may be a hidden meaning. This is when the actor has to look for something which is frequently spoken of as the subtext.

Suppose the line is a very simple statement, 'The train goes at three o'clock.' There could be a number of reasons for the statement. Quite simply it could be the answer to a question. But suppose that the information that you give is not correct. There could be any number of reasons for this. You tell a lie because you want someone to miss the train. You pretend it goes later because you want the person to stay with you. In these cases the actor has to think not just of the time of the train but of the reason why he is giving the information. That will govern the way that he says it. Should the audience realise that he is lying? Should the person realise that the information is wrong? Making clear the implications to the audience depends on the skill of the actor.

Conflict

All drama is conflict. That is the difference between a narrative and a play. A narrative is related by a single person and nobody disputes the story; it is happening in the past. In a play everything is happening in the present. Do not confuse conflict with aggression. A scene can be a fierce quarrel or it can be a gentle and loving persuasion and refusal. It can take the form of a game, but in each case the intention is to win that game.

Directors

The director directs the play. In the professional theatre he decides the casting, but in a drama school he is usually guided by the principal, who wants to be sure that each student gets a variety of parts to play. Every effort is made to avoid typecasting and to explore the student's potential capacity. During the first few terms students usually work with staff directors, who give more teaching about the acting process than outside directors.

Intentions and objectives

These are terms frequently used by directors. A character is supposed to have in his mind an intention – that is to say, he intends to follow a certain course of action. Or he has an objective – something he wishes to achieve. Consequently, all his actions are directed towards that intention or objective.

There may not seem much difference between intention and objective. The presumption is that people always know what they want. But they do not always know. Sometimes they are confused.

There is also the possibility of oversimplification. The actor can be trapped into thinking too much about his own performance, and not enough about what the other actors are doing. However, thinking about intentions and objectives can be very useful in giving energy to a performance.

In the passage quoted above (under COMMUNICATION AND SUBTEXT) Lysander has a clear objective – to persuade Helena to believe him. Here the idea can be useful as it causes him to be more urgent as the speech progresses. Helena intends (or has the objective) to convince him that he is wrong. But in each case their attention is on the other person to see what effect their words are having.

Listening

About seventy per cent of acting is listening to other people. Even the leading character usually spends more time listening than he does speaking. So why is he in the scene? Because he is being affected by what is happening and when he speaks it is a reaction to what he has heard. Look at Act I scene ii of *Hamlet*. The king has a very long speech in which he is giving us the situation. He dispatches a couple of ambassadors and deals with Laertes' request. He then turns to Hamlet, and an aside spoken by Hamlet gives us the beginning of the conflict between them.

The long soliloquy that Hamlet speaks when he is left alone is a reaction to what he has been hearing. His view of the situation is very different from the king's. During the scene he has spoken five times and all of these are reactions to what has been said. We see his situation changing before our eyes. He has been hoping to go back to Wittenberg, but he agrees not to go – apparently in response to Gertrude's plea. How much of this is true? Does he realise that Claudius has no intention of letting him go back? The way that Hamlet speaks the soliloquy is going to depend on how he has felt about what has been going on in the scene. Does he hate himself for having agreed to stay?

What you say and how you say it depends on what you have heard.

Motivation

Originally only used by American directors, mostly of the Method school, but became part of our theatre language. The motive or reason for doing something. Ask yourself, 'Why do I do this?' Sometimes the reason is very complex. You cannot arrive at the complete answer in the first stages of rehearsal. Simplify. I do not know why my character asks a certain question. One thing is for certain – he wants to know the answer. So play just that. You may not be right in the way that you are doing it but you cannot be wrong in what you are doing.

Plot and theme

The difference between these two terms is as follows: a **plot** is a series of events that form a pattern, giving shape to a story – a beginning, a middle and an end; a **theme** is the idea, or philosophy, or moral that has been demonstrated by the story. For example, *Richard III* has both plot and theme. At the start, Richard tells us that he is determined to prove a villain and also his reasons for doing so. As the plot unfolds, he manipulates his way to the throne. Once there, the theme becomes evident: he begins to realise that, in manipulating and discarding people so ruthlessly, he has left himself bereft of all friendship and support and is a deeply lonely man. His final soliloquy demonstrates the conflict between his realisation of the ugliness of his life – his loneliness – and his proud refusal to indulge in self-pity.

Stanislavski and method acting

If you want to understand all this there are three books you should read. (Also have a look at BOOKS ABOUT ACTING in the final part of this book)

The first is *My Life in Art*, a wonderful and, in places, very funny book. Stanislavski admits how, as a young amateur, he did some really bad acting. But it is because he was so honest with himself that we now know certain truths about acting. He set out to discover why he could sometimes be very good and sometimes bad. He recorded in his diary every performance he gave. He formed a studio and experimented with various acting exercises.

The second book of his you should read is *An Actor Prepares*. I think it is better read, and better appreciated, when you have done some acting. Stanislavski writes as though the students with whom he is working are all beginners. In actual fact, he never worked with beginners but with talented young actors whom he admitted to his studio after very careful audition. I think he did that because he wanted to be asked the right questions, and because he did not want to waste time. He wanted to work on the theory of acting, and you cannot do that if you have to stop and tell your actors how to project their voices, or how to stand on the stage.

The third book is *Building a Character*. When you are fairly sure of the preliminaries, and have done a few acting exercises where the play and the characters are discussed and the text explored, then it may be time to read this book. You will get a further understanding of what you have been taught so far.

3 Reading and memorising

Much of the actor's income can depend on his ability to read. Many actors earn good money in commercials and dubbing which enables them to take the theatre work which they enjoy, but which may not be well paid enough to enable them to live. However, success in this kind of work needs not only the right kind of voice, but a skill in reading.

There are two kinds of reading in which an actor should be proficient. First, there is **sight-reading**, which is important for the reasons mentioned above. When actors are sent for a part they are asked to 'read cold', which means sight-read, or read after only a few minutes in which to look at the script. This is a skill which the actor must perfect by continual practice. He cannot expect to master the technique in class any more than a student learning to play the piano can expect to practise scales in class. Nothing but homework will give the actor the skill he needs.

The other kind of reading is **rehearsal reading** which also can only be practised by the actor himself. This kind of reading can be prepared by the actor when he knows what is going to be worked on the next day in rehearsal – indeed it should be prepared, because he wants to relate to his fellow actors as quickly as possible and make an immediate contact. This skill is of great value, but it needs to be done properly.

Some years ago, actors were encouraged to carry their scripts in rehearsal until they knew the part. The idea was that this way an actor would become familiar with the character without having to memorise. Far too often, a messy, self-improvised performance was the result. The actor was supposed to be able to discover more about his part this way. But an actor cannot listen to other actors if he is looking at his script. Some actors learn their lines 'parrot-fashion' and put the acting in afterwards – a method which seems equally futile, since a human being is not a parrot. That he should have his lines at the earliest possible moment is important. A director cannot do much with an actor who has his nose in the script, nor with one who is stumbling, inaccurate and taking continual prompts.

At an early stage of rehearsal, if the director has said he wants lines memorised quickly, actors will sometimes dry at rehearsal and, becoming frustrated, will complain bitterly that they 'knew them last night'. But the reasons are twofold. The first is unfamiliar surroundings. The room in which the actor memorised his lines has, in his subconscious, become the place in which he is acting. Next morning in rehearsal his subconscious begins to tell him that something is wrong – he is in the wrong place! He loses concentration and the lines go. For the same reason, actors who have been quite sure of their lines in a rehearsal room will dry in a technical rehearsal. This is, of course, only a temporary problem and will right itself again as soon as the new background becomes established as the right one.

The other cause of drying or stumbling in rehearsal has nothing to do with the actor's capacity for memorising. If he has just been given some copious notes by the director he will be thinking about how to integrate these notes, and for the moment the lines will go.

No matter what method you use to memorise, these moments of memory loss are likely to happen, and, if you know that your homework has been well and truly done, there is no need to get into a state of nerves and worry.

The actor who has successfully memorised his lines 'parrot-fashion' will use the rehearsal as a memory test and feel pleased with himself because he has got through without a prompt. He is unaware that he has not listened to what the other characters have been saying, or been affected by what they have been doing. He has probably made some token indications of grief or joy because this is what his own lines suggest to him. He has spoken his own lines and waited attentively for his next cue. He has not prepared himself for being acted upon. The rehearsal will have been almost meaningless.

Some students copy out their parts. What they are in fact doing is creating for themselves an old-fashioned cue script. It is one way of knowing nothing of the play but the lines you speak! But then some actors judge the worth of a part by the number of lines they have. They will actually count them up and, should the total not be to their satisfaction, grumble that the part is not worth playing! This attitude comes from ignorance and the wrong idea of acting; ignorance, because they are unaware that some of the greatest scenes in all drama are very short. That is, they contain very few words. They are conceived of in terms of dramatic action. It is dramatic action rather than the words that the actor should start by memorising, and that action does not concern only himself.

Rehearsal reading is not the easiest of skills to acquire but it is very worth-while. Anyone who really grasps it finds it of immense help. So here is a description of how to set about it.

Having got his call for the next day, the actor goes over the material and, if possible, reads the text aloud to himself. He then goes over it very slowly. He takes short phrases and, looking up from the text, speaks those words to the imaginary character he is addressing.

Do not try to take up too many words at once when you are beginning this exercise. As you work, take up a short phrase, look up from the script, speak and hold the thought. Keep the thought and the awareness of the character you are speaking to and hold that thought in your mind as you look down to find the next phrase. It is as though you are saying to your listener, 'Stay there, I have not finished.' As you practise you will find that the phrases you can pick up get longer. The important thing to remember is **never look down at the script while you are speaking.**

Many students complain that this approach feels very slow. It is meant to be slow! Professionals who have learnt this way of reading have found it of great value because it slows you down and makes you think about what you are saying and to whom.

So it may be that overnight, as you work on your material, you will make a light pencil mark to separate the phrases in such a way that you can speak them comfortably. Here is a piece of marked text chosen at random from *Cymbeline*:

> My fault being nothing – / as I have told you oft – /
> But that two villains, / whose false oaths / prevail'd/
> Before my / perfect honour, / swore to Cymbeline /
> I was confederate with the Romans./ So /
> Follow'd my banishment, / and this twenty years /
> This rock and these demesnes / have been my world, /
> Where I have liv'd / at honest freedom, / paid
> More pious debts / to heaven / than in all /
> The fore-end / of my time.   III iii 65-73

When you are working you will probably pick up the first four words easily enough. The phrase is an almost complete thought. Think about giving that information, make your hearer wait as you find the qualifying statement – the next six words, all monosyllables. As you work on the piece you will find that you can pick up half a line at a time and that each short phrase is a more or less complete thought, a piece of information that you are giving. After practising this for some time, you will begin to find that you know it. The important thing to keep in mind is: never look down while you are speaking and never speak while you are looking down. This way you will find that you are memorising thoughts.

Think of it like this. Human beings invented language thousands of years before they invented print. At some stage, probably very slowly, they found it necessary to record their thoughts. Since they had no mechanical means of recording sound, all they could do was make marks on a flat surface. They invented writing. Depending on the civilisation and the language, these marks can go from left to right, from right to left, or from top to bottom. The words are there, but they remain silent until a reader translates them back into sound. Of course, we have been trained to read fast and silently, which is in many ways a great pity because we no longer immediately hear the sound of the word as we read it. This fast, silent reading can be almost a hindrance to an actor who needs to hear a play as he reads it. You sometimes hear an actor say of a poorly written play, 'It doesn't come off the page.'

We need to translate the words back into sounds, and the most logical way to do it is to direct these sounds – those words – where they are meant to go. Memorise the thought, not the print. Actors who memorise print will often dry at the early stages of rehearsal, in spite of hard work, and are at a loss to account for this happening. They have visualised the lines mentally, moving from left to right. Consequently, the brain must redirect them in rehearsal, which slows the process down. Working thought by thought, we give our brains more accurate information.

Rehearsals are for getting into contact with your fellow actors as soon as possible, for discovering what the play is about.

I have encouraged students and professional actors to use this form of rehearsal reading and they have found it marvellously helpful. Slower to start with, but quicker and more secure in the long run.

4 Breathing

In Jean-Louis Barrault's book *Memories for Tomorrow* (Thames & Hudson, London 1974) there is an amazing description of the breathing process, much of which he learnt from Artaud. His book is daunting, because of what his brilliant and extraordinary mind has made not only of his artistic career but of his personal and spiritual life. You have to grow into the book. It may take years but that does not lessen its value: it is a marvellous book. But it does somehow leave one with the feeling that life is not fair. Why should a human being be so phenomenally gifted – artistically, intellectually, physically – and yet have the ability to be a totally unselfconscious, warm-hearted human being?

I saw his *Rabelais* at the Old Vic. Some of the audience were seated on the stage. I was among them. Waiting for the performance to start, I was suddenly aware that Jean-Louis was beside me. In shirt and dark trousers he was mingling with the audience, talking to those he knew, answering questions from those he did not, laughing and chatting. If you want to know what Shakespeare was like as a person, read Barrault's book. I think Shakespeare must have been very like Jean-Louis Barrault.

But to return to our everyday struggle with the problems of acting – and in particular breathing – it is curious that something we do from the moment of birth to the instant of death, something we do all the time without thinking about it, should present difficulties when we come to act. Of course, it is not only in acting that breathing has to be thought about. In swimming, running – any sport – breathing has to be considered consciously and controlled for a particular purpose. In the theatre, from a purely pragmatic point of view, correct breathing allows us to communicate our thoughts and feelings to every member of the audience, no matter how large or how small the space in which we are playing.

Your voice teacher will give you instruction in detail to understand how, physiologically, your voice works. You will be given exercises to strengthen and improve it. But it is not always easy in the early stages of training – when you have so many other classes to attend – to remember, when you get home at night, just what has been said. (You may not even understand your own hastily scrawled notes.) It may be difficult to link what you have been taught with your experience in rehearsal.

It was said of the great Sarah Bernhardt that she could speak fifteen alexandrines in a single breath. Who cares? What matters was what effect it had on her audience. If she made them feel for the character by doing it – splendid. If she merely provoked a burst of applause for her virtuosity, it meant no more than when a singer puts in a few extra trills or hangs on to a top note for unendurable seconds at the end of an aria.

Think of it like this. Since life itself begins with a breath and when we stop breathing we die, it stands to reason that we cannot perform any action, no matter how simple, without taking breath in to do it.

Now, suppose you do not agree with me about the statement. Imagine we are talking together – what would happen?

If you were considering it, you would be silent, breathing quietly, normally, unselfconsciously. Then, as you felt the need to respond growing in you, you would probably take a deep breath, hold it for a few seconds as you waited for the words to come, and then slowly say, 'No, I don't agree with you' and you would allow the thought to go on for another few seconds before taking another breath to explain why you disagreed.

It might happen that even while I was talking you felt that you were in total disagreement. So you would probably take a strong breath even before I had finished speaking, ready to say at once, 'No, I don't agree with you.' And the thought would continue; you would pressure me with it until you were ready to take another breath, ready to say once more, 'No, I don't agree with you.'

But suppose you thought what I had said was silly and trivial. You would be irritated and take just enough breath to say dismissively, 'No, I don't agree with you', and instead of pressuring me with your opinion you would let your mind go to something quite different.

Try out each of those imagined situations. Reading about something, or being told of it, does not mean that you know it. You must experience it yourself in order to remember, and have use of it when needed. We are told that we learn by experiences, but we are rarely told how to look for them and examine their worth.

In each case, what you have been doing is breathing to express a feeling, but the feeling did not originate in you – it was in reaction to something I had said.

'All acting is reacting.' I have long forgotten who said that, but it is true. In other words, 'All feeling is responding' – responding, that is, to a person or a situation. If we wake in the morning to the sunlight streaming into the room and realise it is a holiday, we take a deep breath, give a sigh of satisfaction and maybe go to sleep again, or take another breath as we decide to go for a swim. Or maybe we wake up in winter in a dark room to the sound of an alarm. In which case we reach out, switch off the clock, take a breath and say to ourselves, 'Oh, hell!' In each case, we have taken a breath to express a reaction.

It would seem that something like this happens: We become aware of a situation, an atmosphere, a person, through one of our five senses – sight, hearing, touch, taste, smell. Each of these senses can send a signal up to the brain, which records that feeling and says, 'pleasure', 'pain', 'disgust', or however it interprets the message it has received. It then sends a message to the diaphragm and tells it to take a breath and make an appropriate noise to express what the nerve ends have told it. The noise may be a grunt, or a shout or a flow of words expressing precisely what has been felt.

I feel, but I do not feel in the abstract. I feel in response to something, however trivial. I cannot exist without feeling, without some reaction to the messages my senses are sending out to my brain. Every conscious moment of my life, the brain is sending messages to my breathing apparatus, telling it how to respond to these stimuli.

I live in response to the world around me. I breathe in response to that world. So, acting is living. Living is breathing. I breathe as the character I am playing breathes. I breathe to express his reaction – his actions. I feel his feeling, his reacting.

Acting is reacting.

5 Centre and being centred

Another American import into our theatrical language. One hears these words frequently in any comment on an actor's work. Was he, or was he not, rightly centred? It seems to apply not only to a physical, but to a mental and emotional existence. Many students in the first weeks of their training become confused about what is meant, because members of staff do not seem to be using the expression to mean the same thing. There may be little opportunity to get the matter clearly explained and, consequently, quite a long time before the student understands and is able to make use of this most important aspect of acting.

My own feeling about being centred is that when I begin to rehearse I think of my body as an instrument. Whether sitting for a reading, or standing for a blocking rehearsal, I like to find myself in a state of preparedness – my weight on the balls of my feet, my spine at its full length, my head and shoulders free. I know that although my nerve centre is in my brain, it feels as though it is in my diaphragm. I know that is where I feel any emotion, although only in extreme cases when great feeling is involved am I aware of sensation in that part of my body. Fear, shock and anxiety can cause me to feel physical pain. Most students remember the knotted-up feeling when sitting for an exam. Great joy can cause one to take huge breaths of delight. When I start acting I like to be in a state of dynamic repose. I am relaxed in the sense that I am not doing anything, but I am in a state of expectation. Observe a cat or a dog sitting in a window watching what is going on in the street. The creature is perfectly still but not tense. He is alive, watching for something to happen. That for me is being centred.

This state has long since ceased to be something consciously thought about. Training has taught me to adopt automatically a state of physical and mental stillness. I am no longer myself. I am in a state where feeling can happen. I am in the process of beginning to live and breathe as someone else.

6 Naturalism and reality

'Everything in acting should be larger than life and twice as natural.'

This is one of those absurd sayings that conveys a truth. It is one way of thinking about acting.

Think of the comments people make on what is acknowledged to be a fine screen or stage performance. Because the remarks range so widely, you might think that they had not all seen the performance, until you realise that most of us have a stock phrase or two which we use to express approval of something which has impressed us but which we have not thought about in any precise way. After all, not many of us are going to write a critical article about what we have witnessed, so we simply say, 'it was great' or, 'I heard every word he said' or, 'I was bowled over'; 'She seemed so real', 'She was so natural', 'She had such power'; 'I believed every word he said', 'I just can't talk about it', 'It was so simple'. You may find all these kind of things said of the same performance. You may hear some derogatory remarks as well, but – though there may be disagreement about the interpretation – no one says that they could not hear, or that the performance was underplayed. In terms of size (the ability to reach the audience) the performance has been a success.

Often actors do not want to do what the director asks, on the grounds that it does not seem natural. They make the mistake of thinking that the truth is what seems natural to them, not what is natural to the character. They do not realise that a good naturalistic play is life as it is lived with all the boring bits left out, and with all the interesting parts tightened up and given a shape – all of which makes the meaning clearer.

Many modern playwrights have made plays about characters who, uneducated and having a limited amount of words, rely on the slang and the phraseology of their social background. Such writers – those who have an ear for the rhythms of human speech – create something that is not only stimulating to listen to, but gives us the deep feelings of their characters. Superficially, the plays of these play-wrights are easy to play. It seems that all that is needed is to be 'natural'. This is where you have to think about the little aphorism with which I began.

When we speak naturally in our everyday lives we are rarely wanting to make ourselves heard at a distance of more than a few feet. So we have to evolve a technique which enables us to be heard in a large space. Speaking for the microphone is also a technique that has to be practised. All the microphone does is to improve the volume. It does not improve the clarity.

The camera exaggerates. That excellent film actor, Michael Caine, has said, 'Show everything, do nothing.' Another splendidly helpful saying. Excellent. But you have to work to discover what it is that you have to show.

7 Energy

You need more energy.
You need more pace.
You need more variety.
You need to do it faster.

These are phrases that you are likely to hear frequently in rehearsal. The director may well be right when he uses one, but unless you know how to cope with what he has said, to understand what he really means, any of these little phrases can be a kiss of death to your performance. It is not the director's job to tell you in detail what he means. It is more than likely that he thinks you have learnt it from a pre-vious director or in an acting class. Anyway, he does not have the time. Directing a play, especially one with students, is not just a full-time job. The director must put in overtime from day one. Since all his cast are inexperienced, he has to expend that much more effort in guiding them through the play. So of course he must make use of the shorthand that is employed in this kind of theatre, and trust that students, even if they do not completely understand, will use their common sense.

I was once in rehearsal for a play (it must have been sometime in the 1950s) and we had a girl with us who was straight out of RADA. This was her first pro-fessional job. I became aware that she was standing beside me. She said very timidly, 'Please can you help me? The director keeps saying I need more attack but I don't know what he means. Can you tell me?'

Attack had been a word used endlessly in my early days in the theatre. So I was able to give the girl a bit of help. But it is now almost never heard. In using it the director meant almost the same – but not quite – as he would have done if he had used the word **energy**. The latter word seems to have stood the test of time and to be really useful. But I do remember a session of criticism at RADA, where I was then teaching. A director told a student that he lacked energy. The student immediately asked, 'How do I act energy?' There were eight or nine staff members present at the critical session and no one gave him an answer. I am ashamed to say I was one of them. If that student ever reads this I hope he will accept my apology, and my gratitude. He made me think. The word energy was new and trendy and we had all accepted it. But it would seem that none of us had thought exactly what we meant by it.

What is energy in relation to acting? Aphorisms are sometimes quite helpful, although mostly they are only a partial truth. I have already mentioned one of my favourites: 'Everything in acting should be larger than life and twice as natural.' When a director tells you that you need more energy, he does not mean turn up the volume. Nor does he want more physical activity. He means that what you are doing needs to be more clearly expressed.

Even for films and TV the aphorism is true. Enormous emotions may be felt by the characters, but with camera and microphone so close, the volume of sound the actor produces can remain very low, yet the strength of feeling – and consequently the power of what is being communicated – is the equivalent of what it would be in a large theatre. This 'strength of feeling' is what we mean by energy in acting.

Activity is not the same thing as energy, although it is sometimes mistaken for it. One sometimes sees productions where the actors are continually on the move – doing things. Sometimes this happens in the production of a seventeenth or eighteenth century play; characters flap fans incessantly, move from place to place, bow and curtsy and make all sorts of odd movements with their arms. It is all misdirected energy. They are trying to substitute what they imagine to be a period movement for the energy of thought that is in the text. In a modern play all this movement is rather more bearable because the actors know how to perform the various actions – making coffee (endlessly in TV), shaking up cushions, arranging flowers, putting the shopping into the fridge, doing the washing-up. All activities which may have nothing to do with what they are saying. Sometimes this is necessary as a contrast to the emotional content of the scene: there are situations in which people will go on with a purely physical activity in a deeply serious situation. If a woman continues to tidy the kitchen when her husband has just told her he loves another woman, we want to ask, 'Why does she go on?' Is she continuing with something that is such a long-standing habit, so mechanical, that even a profound shock cannot break it? Or is she continuing her physical activity as a way of rejecting what she has heard?

In the second case it may seem that the woman is slowing down as the scene goes on: she does not see where she is putting things; her physical energy appears to have ebbed. But mental and emotional energy is not the same as the physical activity. The actress's energy is being re-channelled. It has gone inward. Inside herself she is saying that what her husband tells her cannot be true. She is feeling bewildered and dazed, or forces may be banking up that are going to cause a great outburst of anger. Physical activity may have ceased altogether, but mental and emotional energy may be at its peak.

One cannot act energy. It is an abstract − a quality with which we endow our actions. What we must consider are the contrasting levels in the expenditure of energy. It is like an engine. Use more or less power, use it with great strength or infinite delicacy, but never switch off! Always, while you are acting, the engine is switched on, silently running as you listen − responding, deciding, getting ready to go into action as soon as the brake is off. You are not going to use that image in an acting situation but you can experiment with it when working alone. As with most exercises, see what it does for you, then forget it until you feel like using it again. You cannot think of an engine or of energy while you are acting. You have to use what means are at your disposal to discover the levels of energy you need − to experience them and know how to call them up at will.

Remember − do not repeat. If you try to repeat what you did you will only produce something artificial. Instead, try to rediscover the thought-process that caused you to feel what seemed to be true about character and situation.

Well, we have dealt with the first of those phrases: 'You need more energy.'

Let us consider the other three.

8 Pace, variety and speed

There is much misunderstanding about the idea of pace. A great farce actor said 'Pace is variety, not speed.' All too often when the director asks for more pace all he gets is more speed − actors gabbling the text. So when you are told that your performance needs more pace, you need to sit down with your text and ask yourself which bits need speeding up because the character feels an urgent need to get on with things, and when the character needs to slow down and listen to what someone else is saying. How much time does he need to make a decision?

What is the overall pace or tempo of the play? A play gets slow when the actors are giving the audience more time than they need to take it in. But if all the actors speak very fast using the same vocal pattern it will be just as boring as if they spoke too slowly. It will sound like a bad word rehearsal, when the actors just sit round and gabble their lines. This, incidentally, I feel to be a pointless exercise. It is to be hoped the actors are not going to recite their lines mindlessly in performance, so why practise them that way? On the other hand, a rehearsal where the actors concentrate and speak to one another quietly, but with speed and intensity, can be very useful.

So the director has said that I need more pace. He means that I am speaking too many lines at the same speed, that some of the thoughts are not quite accurately expressed. Go over them. I could speak that line faster: the content is not all that important, but in the second line it is. That needs a bit more emphasis. Try speaking the first line faster. I, the character, want to get on to what is more important. Then play the second more firmly. Make them listen. So the text is re-examined and the ideas made clearer – to me, to the character and to the audience. Every line I speak does not have the same value. Make decisions about when a pause is needed and when it is not.

It is axiomatic that farce must be played at top speed. This means that the actors must make their characters think very fast. But often in farce there can happen a moment when the leading character is alone on stage with an enormous problem to work out. If he is a great farceur then the spectacle of him thinking out how he shall solve that problem can have genuine theatre magic.

'You need more variety.' Well, see above. By following the approach I have just outlined you will also bring variety to your performance.

'You need to do it faster.' If you rush through your text without thinking, you will come to grief. What is to be gained by more speed? Some of the advantages have already been discussed, but the chief value is that it can stop actors thinking about what they are thinking! If the director insists on faster thinking, not just faster recitation of the words, the result can be really valuable.

Try it for yourself. It is possible, by playing very slowly, to allow a split second or so of one's own thought to get between oneself and the character. One starts to think about what one is saying, to indulge oneself in the pleasure of doing it rather well. The movement in this direction can be so slight that that the actor is not conscious of what he is doing; but when made to express himself very quickly, he often gets back to the original spontaneity, and sometimes finds fresh ideas and subtleties.

A warning. Do not work on any of these directives without taking the relevant precautions. Know what you are doing and why you are doing it. An experimental exercise well worked is excellent, wrongly worked it is not just useless, it can be harmful.

9 Generalising

In the last section we considered the fact that if all the actors speak very fast using the same vocal pattern it will be just as boring as if they spoke too slowly. This might be described as 'generalising': the tendency to play a scene or even a whole performance in just one way. It can happen when an actor tries to play a feeling, and one feeling only, through a speech or a scene.

When asked what is going on, the student will reply quite rightly that the character is angry or that he is upset. But being angry or being upset is not an action. You cannot play feeling (just as you cannot act energy). What you play is what the feeling causes you to do.

Try it for a moment. Sit still and think of something that makes you very angry. Go on imagining it for as long as you can, but *do nothing*. The feeling will go on building up inside you until you have to release it. You shout, you stamp, you kick the furniture, you may even smash something.

Now try it with something you like. Imagine that you have just been asked to play a lead part at the Royal National Theatre. Try thinking about that and keep absolutely still and do nothing. Sooner or later you will find yourself smiling, moving, wanting to tell someone. Again you are releasing a feeling. Expressing it. With each release of feeling was there not something enjoyable? Think how often we say something like, 'I had a good cry, I feel better now' or, 'I got it off my chest, I just told him what I thought of him' or, 'It was so wonderful, I was dancing around the room.'

Of course, if what happens gives you a shock, the effect will be different. Think how often you hear someone say, 'My heart stopped.' One is temporarily immobilised. Then comes the feeling, followed by the expression of it. Shouting, weeping, laughing, dancing about are all manifestations of feeling. We show a character by showing how that character reacts to situations. Everyone reacts differently. Everything depends on how your character feels about the situation. But if you just think angry and try to play anger, the character will just be a type, a cliché, a poor carbon copy of another performance.

Nearly all characters in plays release through words. All Shakespeare's characters do this. Probably one of the reasons that his plays have been popular for hundreds of years is that his characters so often say things we wish we had been able to say in their situation. We identify with them. What Shakespeare does is to put into precise words the variations of what a character feels at any moment in his life. It is what any good dramatist does. This is why, if we are to do justice to such texts, we must not generalise.

10 Improvisation

Improvisation has now become a recognised part of an actor's training. Mike Leigh says, 'Improvisation is something that only happens once. As soon as you try to repeat it, it is no longer improvisation.' Now, it may seem a contradiction in terms that anyone can be trained to invent something on the spur of the moment, but there are techniques which can be helpful.

Not all improvisation classes deal with creation of character and reaction to situations. Much work is done on the purely physical reactions of actors to one another and to the space in which they are working. This work relates more Lecoq, with whom most of our modern teachers of movement have at some time studied, and which is directed towards helping the student to make supple and imaginative use of his body.

Many directors now use improvisation before starting on the text of a play. By imagining how a character might react to a situation not in the play – perhaps happening before it begins – the actor makes discoveries about why that character behaves as he does in the play itself. Of course, actors have always done this. I remember doing it myself, wandering around the flat – if everyone was out – or when doing the washing-up. But we did it alone and in private. Now such experiences and discoveries can be made in the company of other actors. I sometimes have a great envy of the young actors of today and their freedom to improvise, particularly as I know I would have loved the improvised and devised plays of today. This may astonish some of you who have worked with me in recent years when my classes have been on the understanding and interpretation of Shakespeare text. However, even there, a certain amount of improvisation may be valuable, when an actor feels difficulty with the language – because he has been led to believe that he has to use a special manner of speaking Shakespeare – or where he finds the situation difficult to understand. In cases like this, getting the actor to speak the lines in his native dialect, or imagining the character in a present-day situation can help to free his imaginative insight.

There are other kinds of improvisation. The best known is that used by Mike Leigh in the creation of his plays and films. His work, which has become more and more successful over the years, is the result of deep thinking and an approach to acting which makes huge demands on the actor in terms of total honesty and imaginative commitment. Under his guidance, the actors create the characters they will play out of their desires, their joy and their despair, and from these observed or imagined idiosyncrasies a play is structured. It is a long and complicated process which, because of the problems involved, demands actors of great imagination, and an understanding of the difficulties of this acting process. It is not suitable for work in a drama school. Mike Leigh is unique.

There is another kind of play created from the actors' improvisation. Here the director will gather a group of actors and distribute material concerned with some historical event (recent or from times past). From the material supplied, the actors improvise situations and characters, while a writer (who may or may not have provided some of the original material) observes and takes notes. The writer will later construct a play, editing the dialogue and arranging the scenes within a structure that will clarify the plot and dramatise the theme. Caryl Churchill, among others, has made many plays in this way. Working in a similar manner with actors at the Royal Shakespeare Company in the early eighties, David Edgar fashioned a powerful play out of Charles Dickens' novel *Nicholas Nickleby*.

Trevor Nunn and John Caird, the directors of *Nicholas Nickleby*, clearly played a large part in the success of the play from the way they encouraged their actors to improvise around the written text of the original novel. In this case, much of the dialogue and many of the characters found their way into the final script. In another case, a director might take a written text as a starting point from which to improvise, assigning parts to actors as in an ordinary production, expecting them to create characters from the material but changing and expanding the situations so much that the original theme is changed. Some students find this work stimulating, others dislike it because they feel that this is taking them away from their basic training – to search for truth in the text. I suppose the simplest explanation is to liken the process to a musician working out variations on a well-known theme. A strong and talented director will make the performance work, though more of the creative work will be his, not the actors'. The individual actor may or may not be happy working in this way. Much will depend on his feeling for the original text. If it is one for which he has great affection then he may not like the changes which he feels in any way diminish it.

There is yet another type of improvisation and that is the kind used by the famous Commedia dell' Arte. In this form of theatre the actor not only improvised his own dialogue, he also played only one part – unlike our theatre today, where an actor might play a great variety of characters in the course of his career and be praised for his versatility. The actor in the Commedia was Harlequin, Pantaloon or Isabella (there were women as well as men in the companies) and it was not unusual for that actor to play that part for the whole of his professional life. The plays concerned only those characters – rather like a comic strip which follows the adventures of one set of characters and continuously creates new situations and stories in which they can all appear.

The scenario, or plot of the play, was written in the simplest possible way and pinned up backstage. The actors knew what had to happen and they caused it to happen in the most amusing way they could. All kinds of variations, songs, dances, topical jokes would be included. The actor or actress became famous as Pulcinella or Franceschina. The stock character could be varied and be given extra qualities depending on the actor's own skill and personality, but no matter how much he was altered, something always remained the same: if he was Harlequin, he was always identifiable by his wand and his suit of brilliant patches. The nearest thing to this in our own culture and in this century might be said to be in the figure of Charles Chaplin, who, in his early silent films, created the famous character of the Tramp – the 'Little Man' – and played him in every film he created until well after the coming of the talkies. Chaplin not only had his own character but he had a group of actors round him who always played exactly the same kind of character in each film.

The Italian Commedia companies began to form in the middle of the sixteenth century and were soon performing all over Europe. At least two companies played in England (one of them part of the brilliant Gelosi company). They were suppressed in 1780, and for years their work was forgotten until there was a revival of interest in the late nineteenth and early twentieth centuries. We know them today mostly from the famous artists who portrayed them in paintings and drawings, ranging from Callot at their own time, through Tiepolo, Degas, Cézanne and Picasso, but most of all perhaps from the delicate, romantic work of Watteau. Fortunately, there is a splendid book on the Commedia by Pierre Louis Duchartre called *The Italian Comedy* (Dover Publications, 1966 – available in paperback), subtitled 'The Improvisation, Scenarios, Lives, Attributes, Portraits and Masks of the Illustrious Characters of the Commedia dell' Arte.'

It was a brilliant form of theatre and those working in it at its highest level were great artists and gifted actors and musicians, highly intelligent and well-informed.

11 Relaxation and tension

'You need to relax.'

Let us consider that statement. It will be spoken over and over again. In voice, in movement and in rehearsal. You and your fellow students will be given exercises to help you relax.

Nothing first-rate is achieved without relaxation, but again and again the student will ask, 'How can I relax when the character I am playing is tense?'

Most beginners think that the greater effort they make the better their acting will be, so they screw themselves up, strain every muscle, and believe that they are expressing great and very real emotion. Sometimes they will say that they are really feeling it. What they are actually feeling is their own extreme physical tension. If they have been acting like this on previous occasions they usually find it very difficult to get rid of the habit. They cannot believe that they are acting well unless they are conscious of this effort. They have not yet learnt the difference between energy and effort.

Effort is conscious and, one might say, deliberately acquired tension. Of course, the commonest form of tension is caused by nerves – which, though conscious, is not deliberate. This usually manifests itself in a tightening of the muscles of the shoulders and in the throat, and this kind of tension has a very bad effect on the voice. An actor can never be without nerves. A natural artistic dissatisfaction with his own work is bound to overtake him from time to time and it is right that it should: complacency does not make for an interesting performance; nor does it mean that the student is likely to learn and improve. But what causes the young actor to tense up more than anything else is misplaced attention or focus. He is thinking about himself and his own performance and what the audience are thinking about him. He has not yet trained himself to think and feel as the character. This is the work he must do in rehearsal. If he is really listening and being affected by what someone else is saying, he cannot be asking himself about his own performance. If he is really speaking to someone else, he wants to have an effect on that person; his attention is outside himself.

Try to simplify when you begin. Nearly all dialogue is either a statement of fact or a question. Why do I state a fact? Because I want someone to know it. Why do I ask a question? Because I want to know the answer. Why do I give a command? Because I expect to be obeyed. Do I obey the command? Do I refuse to obey? Where do I focus my attention?

All drama is conflict. Conflict is only in certain situations aggression. Sometimes the conflict comes out of affection and fun, as in the scenes between Rosalind and Celia. Sometimes it is an interior conflict, as in a soliloquy, when an actor speaks his thoughts aloud. Here the character is in conflict with himself – his alter ego. Where there is no conflict there is no drama.

It can help to eliminate tension if you act relaxation. Think about the character's physicality. Is he relaxed in his movement, perfectly free and easy, capable of perfect stillness? Is he the kind of person who would not make small fidgety gestures?

Some years ago a remarkable man called Matthias Alexander was giving what we now call a 'one-person show'. In his case, it was a Shakespearian recital. His voice gave out. He was forced to rest. His voice came back. He started giving his show again. Once again his voice gave out. He rested it and it came back. Sensibly, he realised that he must be doing something in his acting which caused the trouble. So he shut himself up in a room and looked at himself in a mirror to see what he did while he was working. He saw that when he spoke as he did in everyday life there was no tension, but when he began to speak as he spoke on stage, he threw his head back, tensed the muscles of his neck and pitched his voice in a way he thought suitable for theatrical performance. Although this had meant that he had been enormously successful with his audience, he realised that for him it had been totally destructive. This discovery fascinated him and he began to realise that many people, not just untrained actors like himself, misused their bodies and suffered strain and discomfort because of it. He gave up acting to study the use of his body. He became world-famous, and today singers, actors, athletes – almost anyone suffering from acute tension or some kind of pain that they cannot account for – will go to an Alexander teacher. He wrote many books and books have been written about him.

He watched acrobats and singers, animals and children. What he realised was that much of the tension and the misuse of our bodies came from a lack of economy in our movements. We so often use more muscular effort than is necessary. Going upstairs we drag on the banister. It is not necessary, our legs can do the job. We heave ourselves up from a chair using the arms. Again, not necessary. The feet, rightly positioned, and the legs can do the work.

Years ago, actors did not talk of relaxation, they strove to acquire what they called **repose**. This is a quality of dynamic stillness. Look at a cat or a dog sitting and looking at the scene in front of it. Only its eyes move. When the creature or object in which it is interested moves out of its field of vision the animal will move its head, but only its head, and just enough to keep the object in sight. It is not relaxed, in the sense that it is not floppy. Its body is still, because it is concentrating on something outside itself. That kind of stillness is the actor's most wonderful asset.

Students can often gain a good degree of relaxation in voice or movement class, but are not always able to make use of it in an acting situation. It is less difficult in class because you are consciously trying to relax. In a rehearsal situation the problems of characterisation and trying to carry out a director's instructions make for insecurity and nervous tension and, unless carefully watched, this can become built into the performance. The actor has not started to imagine the physicality and consequent degree of relaxation that belongs to the character. How far is the character mentally relaxed? How far does mental tension cause physical tension? Is the character coping with a situation and therefore secure, or is he afraid and therefore to some degree tense? What form does his tension take? My own tension will not do. I must assume the exact tensions of the character. This means I must be relaxed in myself as an actor, otherwise I cannot

make a truthful selection of those movements and vocal changes that will externalise what I am feeling and thinking. This does not, of course, mean that I am
going to plan out what I am going to do, but by using my imagination to discover
what my reactions are as the character, I shall make decisions about those which
are most important and necessary, and scrap the rest.

In the first part of this book we touched on the question of how much an
actor can live the part. Whether it is possible to play a character and not be tense
oneself brings us back to it again – whether or not actors really do live their parts.
The clear answer is no. As Peter Brook said, if that were so, an actor would do
himself untold damage. Oedipus would have to put out his eyes and Othello stab
himself. But we believe that we are living a character. Acting is a kind of self-
hypnosis. The great eighteenth century actress Sarah Siddons said that she went
into a trance when she was acting. She would never allow anyone to speak to her
in the dressing-room during a performance, nor in the wings during it. Many
great performers need this deep concentration and can suffer considerable upset
if anything happens to break it. They will become almost completely unconscious
of anything that is happening outside the play. But there is always a part of the
mind – the part that has been an active monitor in rehearsal – which has now
retreated almost to the subconscious but which is telling the actor where the
audience is, where the lights are, whether he is being heard by the audience. His
technical expertise has become so much a part of himself that he no longer has to
think about it. Remember, 'Thy danger chiefly lies in acting well.' That quotation at the beginning of this book is the best explanation of the acting experience
that I have ever come across.

But back to tension. Though we dislike it when actors are tense, we praise the
dramatic tension in a scene. We mean nothing derogatory when we speak of a scene
being tense, indeed we complain if the tension is too slack. Confusing, isn't it?

So what is the actor to do when he is asked to play a scene where the character is very tense? First of all, consider what is causing the character to be tense.
What is the situation in which he is involved and how does he deal with it? How
does the tension manifest itself? The physical manifestation of a character is very
revealing. Is it shown by restless twitching movements or by an extraordinary
stillness? Where is the attention being directed? This is why it is important to
start creating a physical entity for the character as soon as possible. Is he or she
relaxed in everyday life? Some people appear to be relaxed but show an inner tension in sharp and edgy speech. Others will appear perfectly serene but reveal a
hidden anxiety by overreacting to sudden noise.

It is helpful to invent some little scene like the following:

A tired and overworked housewife has a row with her husband. She comes
back from shopping, having had to drag a shopping trolley uphill for a long way.
When she comes in she has been building up anger and resentment all day. She
slams the door shut, stamps to the sink, fills the kettle, cannot find the matches,
empties the shopping trolley on the floor until she finds the matches she has
bought, lights the gas underneath the kettle, finds a cigarette, lights it, gets milk

from the fridge, shoves a few purchases in, slams door, makes tea, finds a mug, rinses it under tap, pours tea, drags on cigarette, relaxes deliberately, drinks tea, tries to face her problem calmly, hears footsteps outside, listens (moment of indecision), decides to keep still and play it cool. The husband enters.

Tension. Total stillness. Both are physically relaxed but there is terrific tension in the scene. The characters are tense, not the actors. The woman's mind sends a message to her diaphragm and she takes a breath – her only action. She says, 'Where the hell have you been?' The husband does not answer but walks towards her. She is afraid he is going to hit her. Physical tension.

From behind his back he produces a peace offering – a box of chocolates. She relaxes, smiles, gets up, touching him as she moves to get another mug, pours him some tea, reaches for chocolates, cannot get the cover undone, bites the corner in frustration, grins at her husband, relaxes and smiles as she watches him do it for her and give it back.

If you want to extend the tension, imagine it is not the husband who comes in but a man who is wanted for murder. You can vary the scene and the characters as you please. Experiment and discover what causes tension in people. When and why do they relax?

Let us consider Shakespearian character Lady Anne in *Richard III*. What state of mind is she in as she enters? Her young husband, Prince Edward of York, has been murdered by Richard and she is now the sole mourner at the funeral of her father-in-law, Henry VI. The actress will have to prepare for the entrance by considering what has just been happening and what she is feeling. Considering what she has been through she has probably got to the stage where there are no tears left. She gives an order to the bearers that they must rest while she makes her lament for the dead king. The next few lines are full of pity for him, for herself and for her husband – 'the helpless balm of my poor eyes'.

You cannot be tense while saying that. When you are hopeless and helpless you let go. There is the relaxation of total grief. Then the anger rises in her, she takes a deep breath and begins to curse the man who caused that grief. Three lines using the word 'cursed'. Now, remember that any release of feeling is to some extent enjoyable. It is a relief to express feeling. It is when it is locked up inside us that we become tense. Remember that at this time people believed in the power of curses. A woman's only hope of happiness lay in a good marriage. That she should have a deformed child is the most terrible thing that you could wish on a woman.

There is irony in Anne's terrible curse because it rebounds on herself. Do not forget that when you are cursing someone you are asking the gods to put it into effect. Too often the actress plays anger here, instead of what the anger and hatred is causing her to do. Think of whatever gods you choose and ask for their help. Put the energy outside yourself. When you have finished, listen a second or so for their response before coming back to the practicalities of telling the bearers that you are now ready to move on. When Richard enters, do you become tense? What form does it take? A release of revulsion in words.

Powerless in every other way, she can tell the man what she thinks of him. She is not afraid; the men are afraid, but not Anne. What has happened to her has put her beyond fear. She goes into the attack. There is no need to be tense. It is excellent to be able to tell him exactly what she thinks of him. Then, as he tries to soften her with compliments, she can show her contempt.

The student actor, when first approaching Richard III, will nearly always pull up one shoulder, screw up a hand and start to limp. Of course, it is a good idea to think what it is like to be so handicapped, but the actor cannot go through a performance with his body so distorted. His voice will be affected and he will begin to get cramp and feel exhausted. In actual fact, Richard is relaxed! He has never known what it was like to have a body different from the one he was born with; furthermore, he has so trained his body that any physical deformity is but a small disadvantage to him as a fighting man. Though he resents and detests his deformity because he feels unattractive and unloved, he is therefore the more determined to get the crown of England as a consolation prize and to enjoy himself in the getting of it. Consequently, he is not tensed up in any way. In a rehearsal situation, the best thing for the student actor to do is to put some kind of pad on his shoulder and a pebble in his shoe and just get on with it. Richard's energy is nearly always outside himself because he is continually manipulating other people, so he must always be watching to see if what he says to them has the right effect.

One reason why the actor will feel unwanted tension during a scene is because he has not properly prepared his entrance. Frequently, he will do some kind of relaxation exercises when waiting and still be tense when he does go on, because while doing those exercises he has been thinking about being nervous. But the character is not doing exercises and worrying about tension in the period of his life before he enters the scene.

To do the exercises is right and helpful, but not immediately before an entrance. Some time before, certainly. Then start to prepare yourself by thinking yourself into the character. What is he doing and thinking during this period? Whom does he expect to meet? What situation does he expect to find? Remember, nothing is ever quite what we expect. We imagine a meeting with someone. We rehearse that meeting in our imagination, not only what we are going to say, but what is going to be said to us. But it never quite happens like that. There is always a certain element of surprise, of the unusual, the interesting, the disappointing.

An actor will get himself in a nervous state anticipating the difficult scene that he has to play, but the character does not know what is going to happen. The actor must always consider what the character does not know. The character makes his decision about how he will behave from the evidence he has – from what has happened and from what he knows. He cannot decide how he will react to what has not yet happened and what he has no reason to believe may happen. Always think about what the character expects, not what you, the actor, know of the scene that is about to take place.

Do not forget that you, the character, do not even know what other people are going to say when they respond to a line that you have just spoken.

12 Relating and relationships

These expressions are comparatively recent in theatrical parlance. At one time the word 'relationship' meant only a family relationship – brothers, sisters, cousins, aunts. One was related to them. Out of this it would seem came the present free use of the word. One relates to the familiar.

It has become more common to say that one 'does not relate' to something rather than one 'does not understand' it, probably because to say that one does not understand something carries the implication that one may not be sufficiently intelligent. But to say that one does not relate to something or someone is frequently dismissive: it is not worth the trouble of one's consideration. However, it is worth bearing in mind that to say one does not understand does imply a willingness to find out.

Sometimes, when an actor says, 'I cannot relate to the character', this frequently carries a more negative undertone: 'I do not wish to understand the character as it is written.'

The actor may find something in the play or part that he dislikes, not because the character is evil – Macbeth, Iago, Lady Macbeth and Hedda Gabler are all parts actors long to play, and they might all be described as evil in their way – but because there is some aspect of the character, or something in what the play is saying, that the actor feels he dislikes, though he may be unable to express immediately what he finds offensive. Time spent in discussion can usually bring to light a sincere objection to the script or part because some theme or characteristic which the actor feels to be morally or artistically wrong is being presented to the audience in a favourable light.

Sometimes an actor will take against a character whom he realises the audience are going to dislike. Some sensitivity, perhaps insecurity, in the actor will make him wary. Afraid of being identified with the character, he may be tempted into untruthfulness, try to soften the edges, show the character as not all bad, and so upset the balance of the play and make the character unbelievable. The best thing to do in this case is to follow Stanislavski's advice. Go through the part very carefully. The secret of illumination is contrast. Search for the one moment of inconsistency – the moment which is not like any other in the character's behaviour. Play that moment and you can be as disagreeable as you like for the rest of the play and enjoy it.

What has probably been troubling you is that the character is not fully revealed in the writing and, lacking a dimension, might appear to the audience to have only one quality. What an audience wants is a flash of discovery. If it can be revealed a way that none of the characters in the play would notice, then the audience will enjoy it more. You will have given them a perpective on the play, and they will appreciate your integrity as an actor that you did not diminish the character's monstrosity but made them aware of his reality. An actor who can do this kind of thing is highly regarded, and serves both character and play..

If you have been told that you are isolated, that you are not sufficiently aware of other people in a play, the reason is nearly always a lack of true listening. You are listening to others as though you were listening to a radio play that did not particularly concern you. Try in the next rehearsal to listen to other people as though what they are saying and doing is something totally unforeseen and surprising. Allow yourself to be affected by what is being said and find the impulse to respond to it.

We have thought about **related experience** – the way an actor relates to his role. We have thought about the way characters react to one another and to the theme of the play, especially when working on the blueprint of a character. There, with Orlando and Rosalind, Lear and Mrs Linde, we have been examining characters where the relationship – the feeling of one character for another – is clear and strong.

Richard III is a part most actors long to play, the greatest comic villain in all drama. But finding related experience here is not easy. It is wise to read the second and third parts of *Henry VI*, where Richard is seen in relation to his father and brothers, and a careful study of his long soliloquy after the murder of Henry where he makes us understand his grim childhood. He never experienced love and will never give it.

Richard's reactions in the play which bears his name are all fuelled by his determination to become king. He sees the crown as a consolation prize for having been denied love from his infancy. In turn, he denies love to any human being with whom he comes into contact. He derives great pleasure from his skill in manipulating people for his own ends. Consequently, he is forever watching, noting their reactions to him, seeing how they can be used. When they are no longer useful they are destroyed. He has no positive relations with anyone, he simply does not care.

On the last night of his life the ghosts of those he has murdered appear to him. He is appalled but there is no regret for what he has done. He admits:

> There is no creature loves me;
> And if I die no soul will pity me:
> And wherefore should they, since that I myself
> Find in myself no pity to myself?
> Methought the souls of all that I had murder'd
> Came to my tent, and every one did threat
> To-morrow's vengeance on the head of Richard.   V iii 200-206

But there is nothing of the agony of regret that is felt by Macbeth and Lady Macbeth, only a defiant pride, 'Richard loves Richard.'

So, by studying the text and exploring its implications we can find some kind of relationship even with such a 'larger than life' character as Richard, and so make him compelling and fascinating for the audience, allowing them to 'relate to him' too. But there are other characters less likely to be of great interest to an audience because they do not play a major part in the action of a play. They are referred to in theatre parlance as 'supporting roles'. They are not given any strongly defined characteristics and can seem colourless. Actors make the mistake sometimes of playing these parts in a slightly low key – as though the character himself was aware of his lesser importance in the plot. They may play them well and seriously, but without any great vitality.

Let us turn now to *Romeo and Juliet,* to look in detail not only at the relationship between the two 'star-crossed' lovers, but at their relationship with the other characters, and how it develops.

13 Romeo and Juliet

Inexperienced actors faced with these two parts naturally enough concentrate all their energy on the big scenes. They are afraid of falling short of great predecessors. Shakespeare does something wonderfully helpful for his actors. He gives them interesting things to do in small scenes with characters of less importance.

So, when working on **Romeo**, you know how you feel about Juliet, the words do it for you. But how about the Friar, Benvolio, Mercutio, Peter the Servant (who cannot read) and the Apothecary? In all your dealings with them you are governed by your feelings for Juliet, but you are never unaware of them as people and of the effect each of them is having on you. You have some wonderful lines about the Apothecary. What do they tell you about this man, and about yourself? And, near the end of the play, how do you relate to Paris?

This last scene is extraordinary, but because it comes so late in the play it is often skimped. Think it out. Here are two young men, both of whom have loved Juliet passionately. Paris, desolate, wishes to leave flowers and spend some time each night at her tomb. Romeo, who has married her and experienced a perfect sexual relationship, cannot live without her.

Read Paris' speech, see what he believes of Romeo. Then go carefully through what Romeo says. Paris has not understood, so they fight. Then Romeo, looking at the man he has killed, recognises him and remembers what his servant had told him of Paris. Grief-stricken, Romeo had not taken it in. Now comes the recognition that he and Paris are two of a kind.

Romeo's first scene with the Friar is the morning after his scene with Juliet on the balcony. He is relaxed and happy and speaks in rhymed verse. His next scene, when he is hiding in his cell after having killed Tybalt, is very different. It is not such an easy scene to play. It is important to remember that Romeo is very young, that he is Italian and that he is living in a period when it was not considered unmanly to give way to tears. In fact, it would have been thought unfeeling not to do so. But Romeo is too self-indulgent and is strongly reproved by the Nurse, as well as by the Friar.

The danger here is that the actor will generalise. Romeo does what people often do in such circumstances – he takes it out on the person who is trying to make him see reason. For someone in such a situation, reason and feeling do not go together: the more the Friar tries to comfort him with sensible argument, the more unreasonable Romeo becomes. He even threatens to kill himself. Fortunately, the Friar not only takes the dagger away, but furiously compels him to calm down and listen to a plan, which – had it worked – would have prevented the final tragedy.

Despite your mood, it is clear there is affection for the Friar and a deep respect. When you rage at him you do not hate him personally. When something goes disastrously wrong we frequently overreact, insisting that nothing will ever be right again and that life is not worth living and so on. It is probably the best thing that could happen because at least it means that we do not lock the pain up inside us and go on brooding. Like Romeo, we calm down and start thinking sensibly.

If you are playing **Juliet**, how do you relate to Lady Capulet? In your first scene, you both share some feeling about the Nurse. She is amusing you, but you have heard the story before. It is all quite good-natured. It must be, or Lady Capulet would not tell the Nurse to stay.

When your mother asks for your reaction to the idea of marriage, you reply, 'It is an honour that I dream not of.' The line is revealing. Girls brought up in the wealthy families of that period knew from a very early age that there were only two options – marriage or convent. Naturally, most girls preferred marriage. Juliet is, at this stage in her life, a beloved only child. Her relationship with her parents has not been deeply tested and she has grown up with the idea that her father will find her the best possible husband, as was the custom. If the parents were loving and considerate, as the Capulets seem to be, then their concern would be to find someone of the same social background as themselves, with tastes and interests in common with their daughter, who could support a family in ease and comfort and, last but not least, was physically attractive. These are all qualities that Paris seems to possess. Capulet points out that, as a caring father, he has been to very great trouble to find the ideal husband for Juliet – and other characters in the play, even Romeo, have nothing but good to say of Paris.

The line, 'It is an honour that I dream not of', could mean that Juliet is not sure if she is ready for marriage yet. But Lady Capulet goes on to tell her how splendid Paris is. The Nurse backs her up. Evidently in Verona he is greatly admired. Juliet is cautious. She is obliging, but promises not to fall too deeply in love. Nothing has been made final. Paris is 'on approval'. If the Capulets decided against him on closer inspection, then it would be awkward if Juliet had lost her heart to him. There is irony in Juliet's promise. She understands the situation, aware that her parents are willing to consider her feelings, and fondly imagines that she has total control over those same feelings – even when faced with a highly desirable suitor.

So it would seem that in this first scene between Juliet and her mother there is affection and a willingness to please and be pleased. But to date, the most important person in Juliet's life is the Nurse. She has known Juliet since she was an infant. She was her wet nurse. As late as Victorian times it was considered wrong for a woman of good social standing to breast-feed her own child. That was for animals and peasants. But it was important to find a healthy wet nurse, a peasant woman who was due to have a child at the same time as the lady. This could lead to great sadness. Unless the wet nurse had enough milk for two babies, her own child could die for lack of nourishment. However, conditions for the poor were so hard that many women were willing to serve in this way – even if their own child were to die. One father could not earn enough to feed eight or ten children. If his wife could earn extra money by being a wet nurse it meant that some of the children had a chance to be well-fed and grow up healthy. Sometimes, and it might seem that this was the case with Juliet's Nurse, the woman became devoted to her foster-child. In her speech we are given a glimpse of the happy foster-home in which Juliet spent her early childhood. The Nurse tells the story of Juliet's tumble and of the 'merry man' who was her husband picking up the child and making a bawdy but affectionate joke, and the baby's reply. It made history in the family. The sheer joy of that innocent double-meaning! But the child would not have made the reply had she not felt happy and secure. So the Nurse, having lost her own beloved Susan, has become a member of the Capulet household. Her husband she speaks of in the past. He has died, or been killed in one of the many street brawls of Verona. We are not told. In a novel we might be, but in a play there is no time, and anyway it would be a diversion. We are in the present and concerned with the Nurse's relation with Juliet. She greets the idea of Juliet marrying Paris with delight. Like Lady Capulet, she believes he is everything a girl could want; none the less, she praises Juliet for the calm correctness of her replies to her mother.

At the ball, we see that Juliet can command the Nurse. She sends her to find out who the departing guests were, carefully disguising her interest in any particular one. Having fallen in love with Romeo and in the balcony scene arranged to marry him, it is to the Nurse that she turns. And the Nurse agrees to seek out Romeo and arrange where and when the marriage is to take place.

What does this tell us about their relationship? That the Nurse, having lost her own beloved Susan, can deny Juliet nothing. If Juliet wants to marry Romeo, a 'loathed enemy', then she must. In her uneducated peasant mind she may have the same sensible idea that the Friar has. Confronted by the marriage of these young people, the parents may decide to forget the old feud. In the meantime Juliet must be happy.

When the Nurse returns, having arranged the meeting with Romeo, she teases Juliet, holding back her great news until the last possible moment, and Juliet coaxes, scolds and sulks. It is a situation they must have played out together many a time, when the Nurse, like so many of us in a similar situation, has withheld lovely news for the sheer joy of prolonging the telling of it. But the actress playing the Nurse may well feel that it is not responsible to indulge Juliet in this way. Should she not have told Juliet to talk to her parents? Should she not have spoken to them herself? It would seem that she never considers taking such action and that Juliet, knowing how her family detests the Montagues, would realise that it is useless to talk to them.

Both Romeo and Juliet, then, have a sensitive, caring grown-up to whom they can go for realistic advice, and it is to the Friar that they both turn. But as so often happens, his sensible advice is foiled by accidental happenings and the pressure of custom among the feuding families. Someone is killed and must be avenged. In spite of himself, Romeo is trapped. The tragic mess created by mis-understanding, accident and sheer bloody-mindedness leads to the death of four young people, Romeo, Juliet, Mercutio and Tybalt. But it is the stupid feud that is responsible for the situation, a feud so old that no one seems any longer to know what it is about, but which the energy and aggression of some of the younger people – like the servants in the first scene and Tybalt, who is a passion-ate fighter – want to keep alive.

In *Romeo and Juliet,* the Nurse, the Friar, and of course Romeo and Juliet, can all become quickly aware of their relationships with one another and develop them in rehearsal. But let us suppose you are to play Benvolio. Nothing in the play happens because of him. Mercutio and Tybalt both play a vital part. All Benvolio does is try to prevent things happening. But, as his name suggests, he is a force for good in the play. The fact that he is not successful in preventing trou-ble must not suggest that he is weak. Other people may be stronger, but he has the best of intentions when he manages to get Romeo to go to the Capulets' ball. That it turns out wrongly is not his fault.

We are not told how he felt when he discovered that it was at the ball that Romeo had met and fallen in love with Juliet. He could not have known that Juliet was at a marriageable age and that she was a beauty. Had he known these facts he might have been more wary of urging Romeo to go to the ball. Had he known, he might not have suggested it.

But even – or perhaps, especially – with a character like Benvolio, it can be useful to go through a play asking oneself just what the character's relationship is with each of the other characters – exactly how does he feel about them? The fol-lowing blueprint takes a look at the character of Benvolio. It should help to sug-gest to you how to become more aware of your relationship with other characters, and how you might relate to your own.

blueprint a less interesting character?

Benvolio *Romeo and Juliet*

1. Benvolio's first contact is with the Montague and Capulet servants who are indulging in a street brawl. He shouts at them to stop and starts to beat down their weapons. Tybalt comes in behind him, evidently delighted at the prospect of a fight, and Benvolio, ignoring the threat, tells him to put up his sword or help to quell the fight. In response he gets an accusation of cowardice and Tybalt prepares to run him through if he does not defend himself. Followers of either Capulet or Montague appear, and finally the head of each house. What Benvolio tried to prevent – a full-scale street battle – begins. The Prince arrives with his followers and stops it. He is furious, threatening any who disobey him with death, and departs – as do all except old Montague and Lady Montague. Old Montague has a very revealing line when he inquires, 'Who set this ancient quarrel new abroach?' The feud between the Montagues and the Capulets is an old one, kept alive by the youngsters, who just enjoy a fight, and by Tybalt, a brilliant swordsman determined to use his skill. From the first words he speaks we see he means to use his deadly skill.

2. Benvolio tells the Montagues exactly what happened. We, the audience, know what happened. A dramatist does not usually tell the same story twice. It can only be because he wants to tell us something about the person who tells it. He wants to establish that Benvolio is entirely clear-sighted and trustworthy. He is also a close friend of Romeo, since Lady Montague assumes that he sees him frequently. Benvolio responds immediately, and sympathetically reports that he saw Romeo when he was out in the early morning, but that since Romeo was not in the mood for a meeting – had indeed avoided one – Benvolio had left him to himself. He mentions that he was himself in a mood for being solitary, that he was out very early because of a 'troubled mind', but no one wants to know what troubled him and he is not the kind to inflict his worries on others. Romeo's father pours out their worries about Romeo. When he sees Romeo coming, Benvolio says with great tact that they should retire and let him make the inquiries.

3. That Benvolio is someone they trust and rely on is evident by the fact that they quickly leave him alone with Romeo. It would seem that Benvolio knows, perhaps from experience, that parents are not the people one most

wants to confide in, and from what he has heard, Romeo's behaviour has been enough to exasperate any parent.

4. Romeo is in a melancholy mood. Benvolio is deliberately casual, but appears to have a shrewd idea what the trouble may be. Without much difficulty he gets from Romeo the reason why he is sad. It is because he is wildly in love with a lady who does not return his affection. Having discovered the reason for Romeo's apparent depression, Benvolio suggests that the way to cure this malady is to look at other beautiful ladies, but Romeo insists that he will only realise how much more wonderful Rosaline is.

5. A scene later, still arguing, they are interrupted by Capulet's servant, who has a list of the guests Capulet wants invited to his ball. The servant cannot read and asks for help. Romeo reads the guest list. Rosaline is on it. As soon as the servant is gone, Benvolio points out to Romeo that not only will Rosaline be at Capulet's feast, but all the most beautiful women in Verona. Romeo will see that she is no better than any of the others. It is sensible advice: Benvolio has a shrewd sense that Romeo is in love with love, not with a lady.

6. On the way to the Capulet's with their friends, Romeo and Benvolio argue about how they shall appear at the ball. Only Mercutio has been invited. The custom on such occasions is for young men to wear masks, dance with the ladies, flirt with them and then take their leave. This is what they will do. One dance and then they will leave, Benvolio suggests firmly. Romeo and Mercutio argue about love. When Benvolio can get a word in, he tells him not to dawdle or they will be too late. But nothing will stop Mercutio talking, and Romeo is fierce in his defence of romantic love. So the two voices, one of fantasy and the other of romance, luxuriate in their rival ideas. Finally, as Mercutio talks poetically of the wind, Benvolio – the voice of common sense – gets this incorrigible pair on the move:

> This wind you talk of blows us from ourselves:
> Supper is done, and we shall come too late.   I iv 104-5

7. How much the actor playing Benvolio notices what happens to Romeo at the ball is for the actor to decide. He has only one line, saying it is time to leave. (Mercutio has none.) But coming when it does, it suggests that Benvolio realises his purpose in bringing Romeo to the ball has been accomplished. The actor has several questions he must ask himself if he is not just to wander around the stage making up some kind of conversation to have with the other actors. Does he see the scene between Tybalt and Capulet? Is he close enough to hear what is said? Does it matter whether he

does or not? He is responsible for Romeo's presence. Does he notice that Romeo does not speak to Rosaline but seems greatly taken with another girl? Romeo does not know who she is. Does Benvolio?

8. Outside an orchard on the way home, with Mercutio merrily drunk and more than a little bawdy, Benvolio notices that Romeo has leapt the orchard wall. Does he know whose orchard it is? What is he thinking of Romeo's intentions? All these questions are left to the actor.

9. When we next meet Benvolio he is with Mercutio, who, sober now, is convinced that Romeo's absence means trouble with Rosaline. Benvolio does not respond to that, but comes out with something he thinks more important. Tybalt has sent a letter, probably a challenge to Romeo. Though they talk lightly enough, there is an undercurrent of worry about this. Tybalt is known as a skilled and vicious swordsman.

10. Romeo arrives in a very different mood from the previous evening and, in a battle of wits with Mercutio, gives as good as he gets. Benvolio takes no part until he tells Mercutio, who has a taste for the bawdy, to stop, enough is enough. With the arrival of the Nurse, Mercutio turns to teasing her. When she speaks to Romeo, Benvolio suggests to Mercutio that she might be going to invite Romeo to supper somewhere. It is the nearest Benvolio comes to sharing the bawdy fun and he takes no further part in the scene. Does he think that one of the ladies at the Capulet ball has taken a fancy to Romeo and sent the Nurse to invite him? Benvolio would probably notice that the Nurse is respectably dressed and has a respectable servant in attendance.

11. In the next scene, Benvolio tries to persuade Mercutio to avoid a meeting with the Capulets and gets teased outrageously for his caution. Tybalt arrives with his followers. Immediately a war of words begins which Benvolio interrupts with three sensible suggestions. If you must fight, do not do it here. Either talk to one another reasonably or go home! But Mercutio is, in his way, as much of a fighter as Tybalt. Romeo enters and Tybalt turns on him. Benvolio must surely approve of Romeo's refusal to fight – although he does not know the reason for it – but Mercutio sees it as dishonourable. Mercutio fights and is wounded. It is Benvolio who helps him away then returns to announce his death. When Tybalt reappears Benvolio makes no attempt to prevent Romeo avenging Mercutio's death. Would he have fought Tybalt himself if Romeo had not?

12. When Tybalt is killed, Benvolio hurries Romeo away and stays to face the Prince. Once more Benvolio has to tell what happened and once more he tells it honestly.

13. Benvolio has no further part in the action, though probably a director might bring him on with the Montagues in the last scene. The First Quarto has a line to the effect that Benvolio is dead.

Benvolio is important to the play. There has to be a strong, sensible character to contrast with the romanticism of Romeo, the dash and bravado of Mercutio, the viciousness of Tybalt and the hysteria of Lady Capulet. The actor playing him can find his character in the fact that he does what he can. The more strongly he plays, the better.

practicalities

Look at me! I'm being funny

We live in the age of sweatshirts and jeans. Charm and manners are out, but they'll come back. They always do

It's a partner-ship, isn't it?

You need more confidence

Never bring the curtain down at the end of a play. Take it up on the next one

Do as you would be done by

I have to tell you that although her work was regarded by all the tutorial staff as interpretatively excellent, the voice tutor felt that her voice was not yet strong enough to fill a big space, and that much work must be done before she could audition for one of our big national theatres with their vast auditoriums

NEVER TRY TO BE ORIGINAL. ORIGINALITY IS LIKE MURDER. IT WILL OUT

Just be yourself

place your hands below your husband's foot

Don't iron out the inconsistencies – play them!

Never copy the past
Never discard it
There is so much good in it

People are inconsistent

Play the comedy
seriously

We are back to gloves again

1 Theatre behaviour

A theatre school tries as far as possible to follow the same rules as the student will find in the professional theatre. I say, 'tries', because these rules cannot always be exactly the same. The school is not a theatre and what goes on is not the same as in a theatre. The school may contain two, or even three theatres of its own, but these vary greatly from school to school and also, the use to which they can be put varies. In some cases, lack of space means that sets must be built on the stage which means that no rehearsal can take place when the set is being constructed. Of course, there is no guarantee that the kind of theatre where the student might later find himself working professionally has any better facilities than the school at which he has trained. Indeed, some professional theatres may not even be as well equipped.

Anyone who has read *An Actor Prepares* may find all this surprising and somewhat daunting. Stanislavski had facilities available which would be prohibitively expensive in most drama schools of today. He not only had the use of most of the theatre staff, but of the stage management and the lighting operator and crew. For their first exercise, students were given the run of the wardrobe and helped with make-up.

Just as the training of the actor's vocal and physical skills has changed since Stanislavski taught, so too have conditions in the theatre. Although his ideas and ideals form the basis of all modern drama teaching, we have to adapt them to modern ideas and to modern facilities. The present-day student begins his training in the studio, not in the theatre, although most tutors begin as Stanislavski did by asking students to improvise or prepare a piece of work of their own choice. This gives the tutor some idea of the student's own preference and of how his mind works in theatrical terms. What is being looked for is not any kind of expertise, but whether the student has a feeling for truth which he wishes to express, and a pleasure in finding the means of expressing it. Has he a desire to communicate?

The whole acting process is taken apart at drama school. An actor does not begin by rehearsing a great part any more than a painter with his first palette, brushes and paints begins to work on a canvas. He has to learn how to prepare his canvas, how to mix his paints, how to select his brushes and so forth. The music student has to learn what his instrument is capable of. So does the acting student. His instrument, of course, is himself. He must also discover what the art of acting is, what the theatre stands for, in the culture of his time and in the culture of times past.

Most schools are pressed for space. Many have overflowed their original premises and may have to hire rooms in church halls and pubs. Sometimes these are shabby and cold. But this may not be all that different from what the student will find in professional theatre, and if the work is good, these conditions can come to be accepted. A kind of cheerful grumbling sets in, and then falls away completely as the actor's concentration deepens. When the student leaves, he has already learnt to work in tough conditions and somehow, whatever the circumstances, to be on time for class.

Being on time is one of the strictest rules of the theatre: on time for rehearsal, and on time for the performance – for 'the half'. The rule in theatre is that you must be in the building when the half-hour call is given – thirty-five minutes before curtain up. Then the stage manager (who is responsible for the performance taking place) can be certain that all the actors are in the theatre.

In a rehearsal situation, actors should be present and ready to begin the rehearsal at the time stated, which means arriving in the rehearsal room five or ten minutes before the rehearsal starts.

When one reads a book about the theatre of the past, there are frequent stories of eccentric behaviour and of stars being very late for rehearsal, Well, stars are stars, and though it would seem that some do not always behave well, their temperament is tolerated because their name brings money into the theatre. However, I must say that I think most of the great actors of today set an example of good and courteous behaviour. Of course, your future employers – the theatre management, the producer, the director – will not tolerate anything less than professional behaviour in a newcomer. Why should they?

Employment in the theatre is not easy to come by. An actor can quickly get a reputation for being unpunctual or difficult and if he is less than courteous to his fellow actors, thereby creating an unhappy atmosphere in rehearsal, the word soon gets around. Directors talk to one another.

And although no one wants an atmosphere of bland complacency, no one wants one in which the more sensitive actors, often the most talented, are afraid to experiment in rehearsal because of unpleasant comments parading as 'outspokenness'. Comment on the actor's performance is the work of the director. If he is good he knows how to handle his actors. To impinge on his province is rude and usually shows little but the speaker's conceit.

At the end of the rehearsal actors gather together for notes from the director. If the actor has only a small part in an early scene of the play, he may not be required to wait until the end of the rehearsal, but if the director wants to run the scene again then he must be there unless he has been given special permission to leave. Notes may be no more than a few quick words of advice because everything has been said in rehearsal.

Generally speaking, there are always those who will only ever give shallow and superficial performances. They talk among themselves, rustle newspapers or eat sandwiches. The more committed actor – the skilful one, the dangerous one – will concentrate on the play. He needs to know what the other actors are doing. He needs to know what the director is saying. Such concentration is difficult when a scene is being repeated again and again. It can be embarrassing if the actor playing the scene is having problems and consequently becoming nervous. There are occasions when it is tactful to slip out of the room, leaving a note on the stage manager's table to say where you will be when needed. However, do keep a watch on rehearsal so that you do not cause disruption by missing an entrance. With a difficult play, the rehearsal process can become fraught with tensions, which are not improved by slovenly and tactless behaviour on the part of the actors. 'Do as you would be done by' seems to be the appropriate motto: if you cannot rehearse with trivial distractions around you, do not inflict the conditions on your fellow actors.

A great director once said that he could forgive an actor anything if he had enthusiasm. Not undisciplined enthusiasm, which can be sycophantic and silly, but intelligent enthusiasm freely expressed. That can be a great help to all concerned. You will be told all these things in the course of your training but it is up to you to think about what is being said, and the reason for it, and to put it into practice.

I believe that most people enjoy their period at drama school. It is a period when it is possible to concentrate on developing your talent, not as yet encumbered with the difficulties of finding work in the theatre, and free from the everyday problems of life – as far as that is possible. It is good to feel that one is making progress in one's chosen field, but there are always the ordinary problems of one's daily life. Such things are always with us, except for those fortunate periods of idyllic happiness that come from time to time and which seem not always to be the result of personal behaviour. These kind of mysteries are not for me to discuss here, but I do wonder about them.

You may find that your day-to-day life is a bit confusing if you do not come from a theatrical, or some kind of artistic background. (I touched on this in the section in ACTING: KNOWING WHO YOU ARE – ACTOR'S BACKGROUND.) The trouble is that the artist lives in two worlds. There is the creative world, and then there is what most people call the 'real world'. It is not easy for non-artists to understand that for the artist both worlds are real. The non-artist is by no means a Philistine. He will understand and be moved by what has been created, but he does find it difficult to understand why the artist has the need to create. He does not understand that everyday life fuels the artistic life, and that creative work can enrich one's everyday life. Charles Dickens had parents who must have been difficult to live with and caused him much grief and pain as a child, but they fuelled his loving imagination and became the model for his fictional creations, Mr Micawber and Mrs Nickleby, two of the most enjoyable characters in all literature.

And Dickens himself? What kind of parent was he? You can read about him in the engrossing book by Angus Wilson, *The World of Charles Dickens* (Penguin, 1972).You might conclude that being one of his children must have been a bumpy ride.

2 Confidence

I do not like it when I hear a director say to an actor, 'You need more confidence.' Confidence in what, for heaven's sake? You cannot just lay on confidence as you might lay glaze on a painting or varnish on a floor. I hate it too when I hear parents say to a shy child, 'Now, don't be self-conscious' or, 'Just be yourself.' But variations of these horrific phrases are used from time to time by directors and teachers. They mean well but they are just making the unfortunate inexperienced actor more nervous than he was before.

How can you be yourself without looking at yourself? If you look at yourself, how can you not be aware of yourself, and if you are aware of yourself, how can you not be self-conscious?

It is a paradox that many people try to escape into the theatre because they want to escape into a world of true feeling. We are, so many of us, told as children what we ought to feel. We are then secretly dismayed because we do not feel as it seems we should. We are accused of being hard if we do not show enough sorrow when someone dies. But we may not have liked the person all that much. Or we may not wish to discuss how we felt.

If we cry all night because the dog has died, we are told that we are making too much fuss. We are being 'emotional', which can in some contexts be almost a dirty word. Our feelings are monitored and gradually we learn to disguise them. The sad thing is that if this goes on long enough we become conditioned and gradually we come to believe that the disguised feelings are the real ones. For those who have seen the great mime Marcel Marceau, the item that often made the deepest impression was the one in which a man assumes a mask, plays all sorts of tricks, and then finds that he cannot remove the mask. It has grown on his face. It is a powerful statement of this very dilemma. What happens to many people is they get stuck with the self-image they have created.

There was once a parent – strangely enough, this was in Victorian times – who realised that his children needed to be free from any image he might have imposed on them. So he bought a mask. He asked each one of his daughters in turn to put on the mask and answer the questions he asked. He felt that, this way, they would be able to answer more truthfully – a stunning piece of perception for a man of his time. Their answers were extraordinary. From then on, he let them read what they liked and freely discussed with them the questions of the day. Well, it seems to have paid off. Charlotte, Emily and Anne became world famous novelists. The tragedy is that his adored son, Branwell, did not seem to profit by the experience. Patrick Brontë and his three daughters imposed on Branwell their conviction that he was brilliant. (He may well have been – there are people who believe that he wrote *Wuthering Heights*.) But I cannot help feeling that, confronted by three brilliant sisters, he had no chance to find himself. I think he felt he had to be like them but better, much better, because he was the man. Perhaps if he could have got clear away from his family he could have found a way of life that was his. Sometimes, to be happy, we have to be free of the pressure to be successful.

Many students, even after they have got to drama school, find difficulty in explaining why they want to act. Few of them can get further than 'I feel I have to do it.' We hear a great deal today about self-discovery and self-expression, but nobody bothers much to define these terms. Self-discovery surely means understanding what you are really like, asking yourself as honestly as you can what your true values really are. It is a difficult process, and if you are not honest and courageous, you may find yourself trapped into another set of values – perhaps because they are the fashionable values of your generation – that are for you just as false.

To know why you want to act is important. You should think deeply about it for your own sake. There are many people on the periphery of the theatre who are convinced that they could act if they were given the chance. When they have had a drink or two they will tell you that they know they can do it. You finish your drink in embarrassed silence because you know they cannot. They are Walter Mittys, seeing themselves as Hamlet or Hedda, but not knowing a word of either. They are usually quite offended when you suggest that they might learn the lines 'just in case'.

This is a completely phoney kind of confidence. But it is a kind that some-times afflicts actors. It is no good pretending that luck (for example, the luck of being very pretty, which will often get you a start) does not play a great part in the career of an actor. Of course it does. And luck can give you confidence of a kind. You feel that the gods are on your side. But that is not confidence so much as self-assurance, which is not quite the same thing. Self-assurance comes from knowing that you are very beautiful, that you have a special gift, that there are some things that you do better and more easily than other people. I think that self-assurance is probably something that, if you are not born with it, you may acquire very early in life; but confidence is something that grows from a learning experience and from an understanding of life. Sometimes confidence and self-assurance go together, but sometimes too much self-assurance can get in the way of the learning process. Because things come too easily, very self-assured people do not always make the most of their talent.

The great problem with confidence is that it is not a static condition. One has, or gains, confidence in different aspects of one's personality, but it does tend to vary. There are crises of confidence following the break-up of a relationship, or during a long period of unemployment. In the first instance, the affection of friends and their confidence in you as a person is important; in the second, some kind of work that keeps you in touch with the acting world. I think the develop-ment in the theatre of the 'one-person show' is excellent for this reason. Even if it only means playing in pubs – though some of those now have well-respected fringe venues – or schools, or old people's homes, it means that you are working on something creative, keeping in front of an audience, gaining some kind of experience. If you cannot get out and about in this way, then write a play.

Confidence in your technique is something that can be built up at drama school. That never disappears for good. Accident or illness may make it seem for a time that you have lost it, but you will not really have done so. It may take time and be difficult to walk again after breaking a leg, but you will not have forgotten how to walk. In the same way, that part of your brain which knows perfectly well about technique has got it stored waiting for the next time that you use it again.

There is a little story that I have always liked. A small boy went to a priest and told him, 'Father, I have lost my faith.'

'Well, have you now?' said the priest. 'It's a terrible thing, I lose mine about twice a day.'

I sometimes feel like that when students tell me about their lack of confidence. It is just not there all the time. The fluctuations tends to be fast and frequent – particularly with artists. And if you observe carefully you will see that people who seem tremendously confident come in two kinds. One kind seems to lack real sensitivity; the other kind hides a total lack of confidence behind noise and brashness and has a terrible need to be noticed.

3 Criticism

> I have to tell you that although her work was regarded by all the tutorial staff as interpretatively excellent, the voice tutor felt that her voice was not yet strong enough to fill a big space, and that much work must be done before she could audition for one of our big national theatres with their vast auditoriums.
>
> Drama School Assessment

To understand and make use of criticism is of enormous importance to any artist. Some temperaments are devastated by adverse criticism of any kind, others are infuriated by it. These are extremes. Most people are somewhere in-between most of the time and only occasionally deeply disturbed by it.

Many demand criticism – but do not like it when they get it. Charlotte Brontë would seem to have loved it. She was always asking for it from her friends, those for whose opinion she had a deep respect. She obviously found it very stimulating. She wrote long letters either agreeing with her critic or rebutting what had been said. It would seem the process cleared her mind and refreshed her spirit.

In considering criticism you have to make up your mind, first and foremost, what respect you have for the person who criticises you. Do you feel from your observation and experience that they are worthy of your respect? How far do they understand the subject?

Most important is understanding the difference between true criticism and subjective reaction. The first can be of great help. The second, though sometimes upsetting to hear when expressed by a forceful personality, is of no value and must be dismissed. For example, somebody says, 'I did not like what you did. It was not my idea of how Hedda should be played.' The statement has absolutely no value. There is no reason in the world why you should play someone else's idea of a character. But then the critic goes on to say, 'From reading the play it would seem that Hedda has great style and elegance, which the other characters feel somewhat awed by – with, of course, the exception of Judge Brack. You dressed and played her as a rather suburban girl with no taste. One did not therefore understand why Hedda felt she had married beneath her in marrying George Tesman.' How far is that criticism justified? You, the actress, may have had the idea that, though Hedda was elegant, she was really a very big fish in a small pond, and that in Paris no one would have looked at her twice. Now this is an interesting idea, but is it valid in the context of the play? Flaubert may explore this idea in *Madame Bovary* but in the play Ibsen wrote no one doubts Hedda's elegance and social superiority. They regard her demands for a lifestyle far more expensive than their own as fully justified.

In a drama school, where individual or group criticism follows every acting project, students frequently complain about being told so many different things: they have had to listen to voice and speech tutors and movement teachers and those who specialise in acting technique and those whose subject is text interpretation.

A movement tutor might feel that what you did as Hedda did not belong physically to the period and society in which she lived. I myself think it important to remember that women almost always wore corsets before the 1920s. It is not just physically important to realise that women were laced into these linen and whalebone garments day in and day out. They were trained to carry their bodies in a fashionable way; there were endless do's and don'ts about how you stood and sat, and what you did with your gloves, and when you wore a hat and when you didn't. Hedda's body has been trained to the customs of the period and she has accepted them, but her mind and sexual instincts are struggling to get free. So the corsets are essential because they disguise her true feelings. They present the elegant front, which she can use to put down the people whom she believes to be her inferiors. Mistakenly, they admire the image she presents. She, because of that image, cannot value any gesture of affection or kindness on their part. So it is clear that physical presentation has to be considered in preparing a part, and any criticism on the part of the movement teacher may be stimulating and constructive.

In the same way a voice teacher may find insufficient variation of tone and pitch to express Hedda's thoughts clearly to a listening audience. The teacher may feel that it is essential for Hedda to speak standard English, and as a contrast, may suggest that the Tesmans have a slight provincial accent. If Hedda has a regional accent like theirs, the voice teacher might argue, the Tesmans might not be as awed with her as they evidently are.

As a tutor mainly concerned with the text of a play and its interpretation, I sometimes do not agree with the interpretation that the director has put on the play. I ask the students what they were asked to play and tell them how far that idea was conveyed to me. I strongly believe that everything should justified by the text. I do not deny that the director has the right to work out a variation on the play – just as a musician has the right to compose variations on a musical theme. Such work has validity, but only if what is being done or said is based firmly in the text.

4 Originality

I was delighted when one of my students once said to me, 'I was so relieved when you told us that we didn't have to be original.' She went ahead and did a lovely piece of work which was full of originality because she felt free to explore the character, no matter if someone else had found the same things. It did not matter, because those things were true. And the student's truth was unlike anyone else's. She revealed qualities in the character that no one else had played.

'Never try to be original. Originality is like murder. It will out.' At least two great artists who were also great teachers have said something like this to their students. Another great theatre artist, Gordon Craig, once said: 'Never copy the past. Never discard it. There is so much good in it.'

Nowadays actors and directors – not always the best of them, but those anxious to make some sort of sensation – will do almost anything not to repeat what has been done before. One of the most obvious cases is the way in which the part of Ophelia is subjected to 'originality' of interpretation. Like Mercutio's 'Queen Mab' speech, it is thought of as an opportunity for the actor to show off. As a result the play comes to a halt while the actor gives a solo performance. Nobody seems to have asked why the scene is in the play, or how it moves the action forward. I have seen actresses play Ophelia as sex-mad, making overtures to the king, throwing her skirt over her head and generally emphasising the ugly side of mental illness. The actress here is reacting strongly against what was done by her predecessors. Rightly so, if she feels that what they did was empty of meaning, though pretty and musically charming. But the description of her behaviour before she enters causes Horatio to say:

> 'Twere good she were spoken with; for she may strew
> Dangerous conjectures in ill-breeding minds.   IV v 14-15

What is the situation when Ophelia enters? Is the Queen alone except for Horatio? Unlikely at this period. Persons of importance were always accompanied by a train of attendants – ladies- and gentlemen-in-waiting, pages and so on. The reason was twofold. A number of attendants was a status symbol, but they were also messengers in a time when there was no telegraph, telephone or fax. Royalty was never alone unless the retainers were dismissed. The Queen does not dismiss her retainers. So Ophelia, burdened with a horrific secret, but whose mind – through shock – is no longer able to function normally, tries desperately to communicate with the only person who can possibly help her but who is not alone. So the poor girl uses images, old songs, old sayings, anything to get the Queen to understand what she is saying and her plea for help. In effect, she is saying, 'Your son, by whom I am pregnant, murdered my father. What am I to do? Only you can help me. When my father and your husband tried to trap him you were kind , to believe that his madness was due to an unrequited love for me. That was not so. There was something else. My father, whom I loved dearly, was the enemy of Hamlet, whom I love passionately. Now I am pregnant. What do I do? You cannot tell me because that awful man whom Hamlet hated is here.'

Her mind will not shape the accusations that she wants to make. She resorts to a series of images and says that men are all alike, then finally, 'Good night, ladies; good night' and drifts away helpless.

The king and queen are compassionate, but have not understood. Ophelia gathers flowers. Why? There is a language of flowers. Does she come back hoping that the queen will understand this way? When she returns, her brother Laertes is there. Any impulse to go to him must be checked by the fact that he is with the king. Though he speaks gently and lovingly of her, it is clear that he thinks her mad. No one understands. Does the part of her mind which is still working clearly tell her to go on with her pretence?

Laertes is grief-stricken for the girl whose wits are gone:

> Thought and affliction, passion, hell itself,
> She turns to favour and to prettiness.   IV v 184-5

Perhaps it is that last word 'prettiness' that makes for her final despair. In a last song she touches on the death of her father and her love for Hamlet.

Her final word is to ask for mercy on all Christian souls. She knows that she is going to take her own life and that it is a sin for which there is no forgiveness. The last four words 'god be wi' you' are, in modern English, 'Goodbye'.

5 Period and manners

That scene from *Hamlet* is sometimes misplayed through too little attention to the text. But there are occasions when knowing something about the period in which Shakespeare wrote, and about his background, can be of help to the actor.

Consider the scene between Oberon and Puck in Act II Scene i of *A Midsummer Night's Dream*. Before telling Puck to fetch the magic herb which shall enchant Titania, Oberon describes how he came to know of it. He witnessed some wonderful happenings and describes them in detail. These happenings actually took place when Queen Elizabeth was the guest of the Earl of Leicester at Kenilworth in 1575. On the last day of the visit there was a pageant on the lake, with a model of a dolphin so large that there were musicians inside it and a singing mermaid on its back. The music was so beautiful that all the watching crowd became silent. There was a show of fireworks seen and heard twenty miles away.

Shakespeare was eleven years and three months old and Stratford was only eight miles from Kenilworth. What of the lines at the end where he tells of finding the 'bolt of Cupid'? What boy would not have gone to look for it the next morning? Twenty years later, when he is thirty-one and his son nine, he puts it into a play. Did this boy like to hear the story and was he delighted with the idea of the power of mischievous magic? If the actors believe this and use it, the extra-ordinary magic happens. Over the centuries, this small boy that was Will Shakespeare is talking directly to every child in the audience.

It is a splendid scene to work on while you are still a student, for Oberon in the telling of the story and for Puck in the listening. It is a good idea to swap parts so that both get the full value of the exercise. If you get the chance to play it, do not forget that everyone was silent listening to the mermaid. You have to feel the audience becoming still and enthralled as you tell the story. It can be a wonderful experience. Real communication.

I am frequently asked by students to recommend a book that will tell them about the manners and customs of past periods. I have read one or two such books and found them quite useless, because they generalise and lead one to think that everyone in a certain period behaved in the same way. They did not. By far the best way to find out how people thought and how they behaved is to read the diaries, novels and plays of the period. This is a much more pleasurable way of getting your information. Fanny Burney will tell you what it was like to be the daughter of a well-known musician, to know intimately many people in the fashionable world and what it was like to be a lady-in-waiting at the court of George III. Read Jane Austen and you will know the kind of behaviour that was considered well-bred, and what was insufferably vulgar, and what was pardonable because the person had not the upbringing and education necessary to act cor-rectly. Books on manners and customs are not useful because they are not inter-ested in the understanding of individual character.

'Manners maketh man' proclaimed an old proverb. A man was known by his manners. They are a social code, and every class of every period has its code. It was, and still is, important to know the code and to give the right signals. How else was one to know if a man were a gentleman, or a woman a lady? Only by being told that the family was of good social standing – wealth alone did not entitle one to be accepted in 'society'. Not to stand up when a lady entered the room, not to open the door for her, meant that you were not a gentleman. (You did not stand up when a maid came into the room, for she was not a lady – she was a servant!)

In Victorian society, physical contact was to be avoided, except in more inti-mate moments between husband and wife, parents and children. A gentleman gave a lady his arm – she, a frail creature, was supposed to need his support – perhaps did need support when the roads were rough and unmade! He gave her his arm when taking her to a formal dinner. He helped her into a carriage, put an arm around her to dance. He must never put his arm around her on other occasions. Such a gesture was an insult or a proposal. In either case, he could be in trouble. He could, of course, catch the lady in his arms if she fainted, and, as females faint-ed frequently (largely because they were too tightly laced, but also to show how del-icate and sensitive they were), a gentleman could get a fair amount of exercise this way! He might even have to pick the lady up and carry her to safety, but he must be careful not to touch her in a way that could be interpreted as familiar and lacking in respect.

There is a good example of how this code worked in Oscar Wilde's play *A Woman of No Importance*. Lord Illingworth kisses the pure young girl who, instead of laughing at him, or slapping his face, runs screaming into the drawing room demanding to be saved and, as a result, the pure young man threatens to kill Lord Illingworth! A girl who flirted and permitted what was known as certain familiarities was considered to be 'fast' and soon got an undesirable reputation which lowered her value in the marriage market. The girl a man married must be pure.

It is difficult for young people today to understand these values. But it is important to realise that not everyone lived by them. (Male members of the royal family did not, for a start.) At any period, if you were royal or an aristocrat, and if you had money, you could do more or less what you liked. It was the class just below this in which morality was not merely talked about, but acted upon. Lady Caroline Lamb (a married lady) could chase Lord Byron all over London and make hysterical scenes in public. She got a bad press but was not ostracised by her own kind. In *Pride and Prejudice*, when Lydia Bennet (aged sixteen) elopes with the ne'er-do-well Wickham, the family goes into shock. When the tactful Mr Darcy uses his wealth and influence to get the young couple married, Elizabeth begin to think more favourably of him.

I have quoted a real situation and an episode from a novel to illustrate what I mean. There are numerous biographies of Lord Byron. The behaviour of the somewhat unbalanced Lady Caroline is well chronicled. But it is the work of a gifted novelist, a gentlewoman, Jane Austen, the daughter of a clergyman living a remarkably unsensational life, who brings inner life to her characters. Lydia Bennet is no passionate, hysterical near-intellectual like Lady Caroline, and Wickham is certainly no aristocrat who happens to be also a poet of genius.

Nevertheless, Lady Caroline, for all her appalling behaviour, would probably have been shocked if a gentleman had not stood up when she entered the room. Standing up when a lady entered the room and remaining standing until she was seated was of enormous importance because it showed respect. Men were supposed to respect a woman. The fact that they denied her the right – except in certain circumstances – to her own property or to the benefits of a good education, and the fact that the marriage service insisted that she should vow to obey her husband, was not thought to show a lack of respect!

Many actresses playing Kate in *The Taming of the Shrew* have trouble with the famous last speech – of which there have been many interpretations. The problem is that the speech is rooted in its period. Katherine is talking about problems that are no longer current. Conditions of life at that time demanded that a woman should behave as Kate eventually does:

> ...place your hands below your husband's foot;
> In token of which duty, if he please,
> My hand is ready, may it do him ease.   V ii 177-179

When it came to this moment in a performance I witnessed years ago, the actor playing Petruchio did something wonderful; he bent forward and, as Catherine's hand came down beneath his shoe, his hand was under hers. When I talked to him later he said, 'It's a partnership, isn't it?'

How is the student in a drama school to understand these things? First and foremost is the need to understand to what class the characters belong. The wealthy and aristocratic could survive scandal, but the gentry and middle-class folk of whom Jane Austen writes could not tolerate it. A woman who had 'sinned' was 'cut' (ignored, in other words) when encountered out of doors.

Hopefully, you will have a tutor who can explain some of these complications. But no tutor, however brilliant and erudite, is a substitute for your imagination. He can tell you what it was like, he can suggest emotional attitudes, but only you can imagine the experience.

Senior tutors can be very helpful, as can older friends and your own grandparents. They remember the clothes they had to wear, and what they were allowed and not allowed to do. A great-grandmother may produce a pair of kid gloves which reach above the elbow, and explain that she wore them to her first ball. One wore elbow-length gloves with full evening-dress, but not with the kind of dinner-dress one wore for family occasions and when dining at home. Gloves were very important and seem, until recent times, to have been a status symbol, since they had to be made from some kind of leather: cotton gloves were worn by the lower classes; wool gloves, for warmth, by the working classes and children. The upkeep of gloves and stockings was hard work, as they needed to be continually cleaned and repaired. You will find from reading Victorian and Edwardian novels that a woman's character, social status and financial situation is assessed by the fact that however neatly dressed she is, her gloves are darned! A family photograph album can be a mine of information. So can old magazines, back numbers of *Punch* and *The Strand,* and of course *The Illustrated London News.* Some libraries have bound copies of these publications and will bring them out for you on request.

It can be amusing to realise that what was 'good taste' in a certain period and a certain society could a few years later be thought tasteless and vulgar. For example in *An Ideal Husband* Oscar Wilde talks of Lady Chiltern's 'pink paper'. By the 1920s pink writing paper was considered common and only servants used it for their letters.

It is fascinating to discover such details, but what is more interesting is that if you do not know the period in this sort of detail, it is not only not possible to get the correct social behaviour right, but it is also impossible to get it wrong in the right way! That is, you cannot know what would constitute bad manners or insulting behaviour unless you know what would be considered good manners in the society in which you are living. Situations in comedies, and especially in farces, frequently depend on a character saying, doing and wearing the wrong thing. Extreme snobbishness is the target of much satirical comedy, but it is important that the actors understand what is being satirised. Much fun is made of the 'fop' – male and female – in Restoration comedies, but there should be a very great difference between the clothes these characters wear and those worn by the elegant characters who are often amused by the fops but disdainful of their behaviour.

As well as being an excellent play, Etherege's *The Man of Mode* is a mine of information about the social values of this period. The fops are affected. They not only wear ludicrously elaborate clothes which they believe to be the height of fashion, but they adopt mannerisms of speech and behaviour which can be quite ridiculous. A glance at some of the satirical prints of a period will give some idea of the absurdity of certain fashions, but a study of the portraits of the same period will show quite clearly what sensible people wore and when they wore it. In any age, there are people whose dress and behaviour is intended to amaze and attract attention, but there are also those who show real charm and elegance.

Period novels not only deal with the romantic and emotional problems of the characters, but with their money worries and the efforts they adopt to 'keep up an appearance'. Do not only read the classics – excellent period novels – but read some of the bad ones if you can find a copy. Bad novels tell us a different kind of truth. How people fantasised about themselves. And, of course, there are plenty of such novels still being written – the sensational best-sellers, published in paperback, crowd the shelves of newsagents and airport bookstalls.

What one needs to know in dealing with a comedy, a farce or any other play of a past period, is the values that belong to that period. One must be aware when a social misdemeanour is a matter for ostracism and suicide, and when it is a matter for mockery and laughter.

6 Costume

It is a wonderful feeling wearing a splendid costume, one that is magnificent in itself and which truly expresses the character for whom it was designed. A costume that is not right, no matter how spectacular it is to look at, can be strangely undermining. The reason is, of course, that it is the designer's idea of the character, not the actor's.

Dressing up is something in which most human beings take delight. One's appearance makes a statement about oneself – one's social status, one's taste, one's income. Uniforms make a statement about status, but they also make a statement about belonging. A uniform can indicate rank; it can also say something about an individual's quality and lifestyle; and it can hide all these things, making the individual one of a group, no one better than another: the Chinese workforce is a good example, with their simple black overalls and white shoes.

But there is this thing called 'fashion' which causes differences, sometimes grotesque, in what people decide to wear. Formal clothes have ceased in many ways to be obligatory now. In the 1930s one could not sit in the stalls or in the dress-circle of a theatre except in evening dress. Nowadays, one of the few events for which people still feel it necessary to dress up is a wedding. Even the most revolutionary spirit will appear in clothes suitable to the occasion and more like those worn by other guests. It would seem to be a gesture – a visible gesture – of goodwill to the marrying couple.

People express themselves by what they wear: there are those who slavishly follow fashion while at the same time protesting that they hate uniform; and there are those who follow their own taste, regardless of what their incomes will allow. When considering the costume for a character these qualities have to be considered. At drama school, most of one's early acting exercises are done in a workshop situation and without costume, except for what the actor can himself provide; or, if it is a period play, cloaks and petticoats may be on loan from the wardrobe.

Some drama schools are insistent about students bringing proper practice dress when they start the course. Other schools indicate what is required on the prospectus, but do not have 'kit inspection' when students arrive. So when their director wants practice gear worn for rehearsal, or for a final presentation, it turns out that the students either have almost nothing, or that what they have brought is unsuitable and what they end up wearing is a hotchpotch of odds and ends. This is a situation that can make for confusion and discontent.

Simplicity is not a bad thing. Stanislavski wrote of the young actor's eagerness to have wonderful costumes. He laughs at his young self for imagining that if only he had something splendid to wear, his performance could not fail to be splendid. Students long for the day when they can get into a costume. Tutors, on the other hand, feel that if they are allowed to use costume too soon, they will not concentrate on the inner life of the character and certainly this is true of actors who concentrate on the exterior presentation. A fine effect is made, but the truth and reality of the character is not there.

Student actors, whatever the situation, need to rely on their own common sense and artistic sensitivity, and their best course is to provide themselves with a useful practice clothes. In the first half of this century, actors had a hamper – a huge wicker trunk – which went with them wherever they played. It contained not only their make-up, but their 'wardrobe'. In Victorian times, actors was supposed to supply their own wigs and costumes, even in period plays.

Actresses in repertory companies had to find all their own dresses, which could be a hideous and crippling expense. When applying for work they would be asked if they had a good wardrobe. If not, they did not get the job. It was the bad old days! Equity has long since put a stop to that and insists that managements should provide costume, but there are still situations – in small-scale, low-budget productions, or experimental and fringe companies – where the actor has to provide for himself. In these cases he will have an advantage if, through his training, he has been thinking for himself about costume and the necessity for a visual presentation. Even in a workshop situation, a lot can be suggested by a pair of gloves, a hat, a cravat, shoes or boots. The manner in which these things are worn by the character can give information to the audience. For example, the way a man takes off his glove before shaking hands with a lady reveals much about his background and breeding.

There may be objections that a modern audience neither knows nor cares about such manners and customs, so why bother? Because it is not only truthful, but more interesting and more economical. The mere slipping off of the glove, the slight bow as the gentleman takes the lady's hand (she retains her glove), tells us of his poise and sophistication. If you are playing an oafish young man, it can help to forget until the last moment that you should remove your glove and then have difficulty in getting it off. It is a way of making a graphic statement about the character through use of costume.

Let us think about the practice costume an actor should have. If you are a woman, most drama schools suggest that you should have a long black skirt, but they may not specify what kind of black skirt. I have frequently seen a girl squeeze herself into a tubular garment, either inherited from her grandmother or bought at a boutique. A good practice skirt needs to be long and full. There has only been one period, the Regency, when women's dress was slim and straight, but there are no important plays of that period.

The best kind of practice skirt is cut circular – a complete half-circle with a half-circle cut out for the waist – a tape to go around the waist and poppers or velcro down the open side. This kind of skirt is versatile, because you can push the gathers along the tape and get the fullness where you need it. If you can afford it, two such skirts are extremely useful. You can clip them together to make an enormously full one to use on occasion and you can separate them and use one as a cloak. The ways that you can drape them, hitch them up and pin them are innumerable. You can suggest almost any type of garment. To go with the skirt you need a long-sleeved leotard. A V-neck is the most versatile.

You will probably be told to bring jazz shoes and, of course, tights, but you would be well advised to get yourself a pair of 'character' shoes. These need not be bought at a costumier's where they are usually rather expensive. What is needed is a pair of plain black shoes with a heel of about an inch or slightly more. (Only in the early part of the nineteenth century and again, under crinolines, were completely flat shoes worn.) The important thing is that they should be comfortable, light and flexible. You cannot tap lightly to show your impatience if your shoe will not let you do it.

Having got these basics and some kind of hold-all in which to keep them, start to make your own collection. These need not involve you in much expense.

- Raid female relatives' wardrobes for bits and pieces of costume jewellery which they no longer wear.

- Look out for scarves and handkerchiefs. A Victorian lady wept into a handkerchief; she did not mop up with a tissue.

- Gloves, invaluable and to be cherished. Never mind how old some of these things may be. Some of the characters you will play may be very poor but trying to put on a show.

- A veil! Very important. Again and again, from Olivia in *Twelfth Night* on to fairly recent times there are occasions when a woman is either raising or lowering her veil.

Now for the men. You will also have been told to have tights and jazz shoes. Like them, and perhaps a leotard for the movement work.

- Get yourself a pair of black leather shoes, slip-on ones not lace up. Once again, the golden rule, make sure they are comfortable. As the tights you use for movement are usually footless, it is a good idea to have a pair of black socks so that you have no gap between them and your shoes.

- The girls have their all-purpose skirts. For you, a similar all-purpose garment can be a black sweater, a good, long one. Also a white shirt and a leather belt, which can be worn low-slung.

- A pair of leather gloves. Two or three, if you can manage to beg, borrow or scrounge them. Gloves were, and still are in some cases, a symbol of status. Anyone handy with a needle can transform a pair of cheap gloves into a handsome fake.

We are back to gloves again. They can be an extremely important part of one's wardrobe. A pair of gloves with gauntlets can do much to suggest the elegance of a gentleman of the fifteenth, sixteenth or seventeenth century. From Elizabethan times to the end of the eighteenth century, gloves of the more expensive kind had gauntlets which were embroidered and sometimes sewn with jewels. (It was gloves of this kind that were given as a token and worn on helmets in a tournament as a sign of allegiance to a lady.)

Gloves were also thrown down as a challenge to single combat. In the nineteenth century, gloves were not so large, but were nevertheless an essential item of dress. It can be quite difficult when no costumes are provided for a workshop production of scenes from, let us say, an Oscar Wilde play. If the setting is a ball, or some such formal occasion, everyone would have worn white gloves.

But if you, the actress, have a pair of long gloves and you, the actor, have a pair of white gloves and you wear them during the last week of rehearsal you will begin to discover clues to the lifestyle of your character. Your gloves are cheap cotton, but your character ordered his kid-glove leather creations by the dozen, made to measure by the finest glove-maker in London. Just putting on your gloves can help you imagine the casual expenditure of money on a mere accessory. Details like this will make you aware of the self-assurance of such people.

I cannot list all the small, useful pieces you can gather and use in rehearsal and probably in presentation. Use your imagination and look at pictures and, if you can find them, at fashion plates of the period. Think about the image that the woman wanted to present, the figures of state the man hoped to emulate.

The great Sargent portraits in the Tate Gallery are wonderfully helpful – but then, so are the portraits of any period. The Victoria and Albert Museum has splendid collections of clothes from the sixteenth century onwards. Nearly all picture galleries have something useful. There are plenty of postcard reproductions of famous pictures, and of famous actors in their greatest parts. All material for the imagination.

As with period detail, novels provide an endless supply of character information to do with costume. Charlotte Brontë is very good on clothes. She loved them, but she knew that being small and plain she would not look good in anything gorgeous, so you find her heroines selecting plain colours and simple dresses – the kind of thing that she herself chose. There is the incident in *Jane Eyre* when Jane is summoned to the drawing room to meet Mr Rochester for the first time. She does not change her dress but she puts on her lace collar!

Then there was the real life occasion when Charlotte and Anne went to London to their publishers and revealed that it was they who were really Currer and Acton Bell. George Smith, having recovered from his amazement, took them to meet his mother and to the opera. They had come down from Yorkshire expecting not to attend any social occasion and had no suitable dresses. But they went out straight away and each bought a new pair of gloves!

7 Comedy and style

Somebody once wrote, I think it was the Canadian novelist Robertson Davies, 'We live in the age of sweatshirts and jeans. Charm and manners are out, but they'll come back. They always do.'

Style is a much abused, overused and misused word. Only one thing is for certain. It is not affectation, although affectation is sometimes mistaken for style. It is thought to appertain to the upper classes and to characters in eighteenth century or Restoration comedy; to those who these days feature in the pages of *Vogue* and *Harper's and Queen*.

A careful study of those two guides to our social thinking should disabuse us of the idea that style is the prerogative of the upper classes. Does 'Jennifer's Diary' figure in the first few pages? No. Her news, and the photographs that go with it, are relegated to the back pages where photographs illustrate social engagements. It is the style of the very fashionable and wealthy – those who are well known in the world of entertainment and the arts – which is featured in the front pages of the magazines, along with the expensively-produced advertise- ments for the right kind of clothes, jewellery and cars. But while some people are noticeable and admired for their extreme display in clothes and make-up, there are others who attract attention by the extreme simplicity and elegance of their appearance. Examine both kinds carefully and you will begin to distinguish between the standards of taste. Jeans and a sweatshirt means that no one can guess at a glance to what class of society you belong. But within the jeans and sweatshirt society a snobbishness has already grown up. The jeans and sweatshirt must have a designer label to qualify as elegant and the wearer must be a certain physical shape to qualify as stylish.

Which brings us to that strange phenomenon, fashion. What is it that makes everyone want to copy their neighbour, no matter how absurd or how ludicrous? What someone a little wealthier, better-looking and more popular wears, others will copy in the hope that they too will look more attractive and be more popular and successful. Usually the reasons people have for doing this are not conscious; they just want to wear what someone they admire is wearing. They are trying to adjust a self-image which they find unsatisfactory. This is something that has happened in every age. As Oscar Wilde says in *A Woman of No Importance*:

> GERALD I suppose society is wonderfully delightful!
> LORD ILLINGWORTH To be in it is merely a bore. But to be out of it
> simply a tragedy. Society is a necessary thing.   Act III

Style in the social sense must be considered by the actor, since so many comedies criticise the social style of the period in which they were written.Style is not merely a way of dressing and a set of physical mannerisms; it is an attitude to life and a way of living it. Not merely manners but morals. *A Woman of No Importance* deals with the situation of the unmarried mother. Here she describes her plight:

> MRS ARBUTHNOT Women are hard on each other. That girl, last night,
> good though she is, fled from the room as though I were a tainted
> thing. She was right. I am a tainted thing. But my wrongs are my own,
> and I will bear them alone. I must bear them alone. What have
> women who have not sinned to do with me, or I with them? We do
> not understand each other.   Act IV

This was what one might call the official point of view, the one that Queen Victoria might be expected to approve, though her son, the Prince of Wales (later Edward VII), had notorious affairs with beautiful actresses and society women, many of whom were married. It was not what you did, it was what you could get away with.

Style is a term which gets applied to any period play, and this is where all too often the acting becomes trivial and affected. Style is not just a manner of speaking, it is a way of life. It includes the characters' beliefs, and social and moral attitudes. There are reasons for the way they behave. These must be explored, and the actors must understand them.

I have headed this section 'Comedy and style' because in the theatre style is usually discussed in relation to comedy. The dividing line between comedy and tragedy is not so strongly marked in modern plays as it was in earlier periods. The two were divided in Ancient Greece when, at the great drama festivals, prizes were awarded for the best tragedy and the best comedy. Human beings have a curious habit in matters artistic. They create rules, guidelines for achieving excellence, and insist that nothing of merit can exist which does not obey these rules. They appear not to notice how many works of genius have transcended them.

In tragedy, the 'Three Unities' had to be obeyed. The work must have unity of action, of place and of time. This symmetry, first evolved in Greece, suited the drama of that society. Where there was no popular press, no education as we understand it, the theatre was a prime source of information. People could discover who they were. The theatre spoke of gods and goddesses, and their behaviour since time began. It told of great ancestors and their struggles with these deities, and of their struggles with each other. It told too of a moral code which, unlike that of the Jews, and later of Christianity, was not in the main derived from the gods (who were often strangely lacking in what men have usually considered a decent way of behaving to a neighbour).

In most societies, adultery is not permissible and is the cause of endless strife, including the ancient world's most famous war – the war of Troy. But how did this war start? With an after-dinner dispute among the gods as to who was the most beautiful goddess. And so we had the Judgment of Paris and a seven years' war and the endless effect it had on so many lives.

All these stories are told in the plays of Aeschylus, Sophocles and Euripides. The gods and goddesses have long since ceased to be worshipped, but the plays are still staged because of their poetry, the philosophy expressed and the ever-pertinent human predicaments described. But had they not been written in the strictly disciplined style of their time, they might not now be so accessible to us. Their message is clearer because of their style, which relates the story with a strength and simplicity allowing for no self-indulgence on the part of the dramatist, nor any peripheral and irrelevant detail.

The idea of the unities and of the tragic form exerted a great influence upon French playwrights of the sixteenth century and after. The greatest exponent of this is Racine, whose use of language, but also of form, makes him extraordinarily difficult to translate. English playwrights, with their heritage of the Mystery plays and the mixture of languages that make up English, did not care for a formal shape until the nineteenth century when the well-made play became mandatory throughout Europe and the Western World. This form itself, however, was bypassed by writers whose work has attained the status of 'classics'. It is important to realise, though, that Ibsen, Chekhov, Strindberg, Shaw and others used the formula of the well-made play to give a basic structure from which to depart as they felt the need.

The student thinking about style must consider the basic difference between comedy and tragedy, since so many plays written in the past make this distinction so strongly. A friend once told me that he preferred tragedy to comedy because tragedy had no ending. He was not being morbid. On the contrary, he found reassurance in it. Another friend, a director, said, 'Never bring the curtain down at the end of a play. Take it up on the next one.' Both meant that the strength of tragedy lies in that reassurance. *Hamlet* ends with the start of the play of Fortinbras; *Macbeth* ends with the start of the play of Malcolm.

Comedy questions social values, while tragedy questions spiritual ones. Comedy is of the mind, tragedy is of the soul. These are aphorisms and helpful because they are easy to remember, but they are incomplete truths. They were more or less truthful until Shakespeare in the latter part of his career wrote a group of plays using a mix of style, both comedy and tragedy together. *Measure for Measure*, *All's Well That Ends Well* and *The Winter's Tale* were for years known as Shakespeare's 'Problem Plays', because in them he completely breaks the rule that comedy must be comedy, and tragedy must be tragedy. In fact, he had been doing this from the start, but had done it in such a way that no one seemed to notice it. As early as *The Comedy of Errors*, Adriana, upset about her husband's behaviour, takes him to task about it in a speech of some fifty lines. In performance, we laugh because the situation is farcical. She is not talking to her husband, but to his twin brother! The material of her speech is not funny. The woman is deeply hurt, and though forceful in what she says, is not unreasonable – anyone believing strongly in marriage as a physical, mental and spiritual institution would agree with her. She is passionate, and far from talking nonsense.

Malvolio, too, is not a farcical character, although he has been frequently played as such. The lines spoken by the Duke and by Olivia at the end of the play make it clear that they take him seriously. But the principal characters in *As You Like It*, *Much Ado About Nothing* and *Twelfth Night* are all what we now call well-adjusted, and cope with their problems with spirit, common sense and wit. They invite our grave consideration at times, but on the whole they amuse us. In the later plays, the neurotic Leontes, the sexually maladroit Angelo and the serious-minded Helena are certainly not there to amuse us.

These later plays end, not with a stage strewn with dead bodies, but with people finding a solution to the problems, and, more than that, finding those solutions in toleration and forgiveness. In *The Winter's Tale* Shakespeare contrives a final situation that is both truthful and magical.

For many years after Shakespeare's death, tragedy and comedy were still considered incompatible. In serious plays a certain 'comic relief' was considered proper, but only for minor characters, never for principals. Great actors and actresses were described either as tragedians or comedians. Though David Garrick was equally successful in both media, it would seem that Sarah Siddons and the entire Kemble family were tragedians of the deepest dye. Both Sarah Bernhardt and Eleonora Duse were world-famous queens of tragedy. Even Stanislavski got a bit muddled when Chekhov insisted on describing *The Cherry Orchard* as 'a comedy, even at times a farce', and persisted in directing it for nostalgia and melancholy. It was played that way for many years afterwards.

Bertolt Brecht gave the best advice on playing anything: 'Don't iron out the inconsistencies – play them! People are inconsistent.' The paradox is that if the actor has perception and sensibility, those inconsistencies add up to a complete and consistent character. Tragic characters are sometimes ridiculous; comic characters sometimes sublime.

So what is the young, inexperienced actor to do? He must realise that in comedy, which is social, a man who has mislaid his trousers, and must appear without them at a board meeting, feels himself to be as much abused by fortune as Lear does in his rejection by his daughters. It is not solely the loss of the trousers (which as a visual effect in the context of the play is very funny) but the fact that he behaves as though the end of the world has come and there is no hereafter! His reaction is out of all proportion to the situation and that is why we laugh. But it makes us realise why the older actors insisted: 'Play the comedy seriously.'

If the actor shows he is aware that his situation is funny, no one wants to laugh. The audience regard such an actor in the same way as they might an obnoxious child at a party who keeps interrupting with the persistent cry of 'Look at me! I'm being funny'.

There have been occasions when a performer from music hall has made a success, not merely in 'straight' theatre but in a classical play. It happened when the great George Robey played Falstaff. When it does happen it is because the act which has carried the performer to success has been based on character, not on the telling of jokes.

Comedy is not just about telling jokes and style is not just a way of speaking. One must ask oneself: are the characters behaving in a way which to them is perfectly natural, or are they self-consciously playing on an image of themselves which they believe to be fashionable and therefore admirable? One must differentiate between natural good taste and elegance and the desire to be fashionable. Look at the portraits of people in the period of the play that you are working on. These will give you the people themselves. Look at the caricatures and fashion plates of the period and you will see how far the desire to present an image, to attract attention, can push us to extremes of behaviour and appearance.

Look at the people around you now. Who are the people you admire, and for what? Usually you will find that they belong to, and are excellent examples of, a particular background and way of life.

Jeans and sweatshirts. Even royalty wear them.

But when the occasion is important, they wear what is appropriate.

blueprint finding the part

Viola *Twelfth Night*

In this blueprint I want to go through a whole part as systematically as possible. There are happy times when one seems to understand the character at the first reading and, as rehearsals progress, more and more things fall into place. But these delightful occasions do not happen often, and they can also sometimes be deceptive.

Looking back on a part – perhaps years later – it can be a shock to realise how much was missed. When one is young, one can sometimes skim joyously over the surface of a part and nobody minds because youth and joy are pleasing qualities. As one gets older, the characters one is asked to play are older, more thoughtful, more sophisticated, their problems more difficult to fathom and their relationships with other people more subtle. Instinct alone will not always get to the heart of a character.

Sometimes characters are terribly difficult to understand. Then there are unfortunate occasions when the direction is not helpful – when it is not good or when you are not given any. Actors frequently complain of direction, but all too often it is because they have accustomed themselves to depend on it. They have worked with highly creative directors who have fed them the part. Good direction is splendid and makes an enormous difference to the performance, but good direction is even better when the actor has done his homework, when he knows what to bring into a rehearsal situation.

I have chosen to go through the part of Viola in *Twelfth Night*. It is hardly necessary to tell you to read the play, not once, but several times – and out loud if possible. Having accomplished that, consider what impression you have of the character from what she does in the play. It would seem that she is a person of deep feeling but that she is also a realist, observing situations and people quite clearly. While sensitive to the feelings of other people, she has a good command of her own. This realism and lack of selfishness is of great importance in the play. That is a general impression. Now go through the play scene by scene to discover if this impression is correct. Use the first person to help you empathise with the character.

Act I Scene ii

The action of the scene is pushed along by a series of questions from me (Viola) and then by a decision I make. Presuming that I have asked myself what I am doing and why I am doing it, I can then ask what information I have gained.

First, though full of grief for my brother, I do not give up hope. When the captain tells me that there is a possibility that my brother may not have drowned after all, I give him money, and later in the scene offer to pay him well for helping me, which means that I must have had quite a lot of money on me when I was shipwrecked. As the captain addresses me as 'lady' I am of some special social status. My father, if not actually acquainted with Orsino, knew enough about him to mention to me that he was not married.

My problem is that I am a girl alone and in a strange country. It is not easy to empathise with this situation when a young girl nowadays can take her backpack and go off almost anywhere in the world. If Orsino was married, then I could possibly obtain a position as a lady-in-waiting to his duchess. However, bachelors do not have ladies-in-waiting. It would be good if I could serve Olivia, the lady who has lost a brother, but she has made herself unapproachable. Then I have the idea of a disguise, persuading the captain that I may well be acceptable as a eunuch because, 'I can sing and speak ... in many sorts of music.' In the final couplet I say that I will leave the rest to time.

Information gained: I am of good family, have some money, do not give way to grief, but can sympathise with someone who would seem to have done so. I am practical, musical, courageous and prepared to see what life has to offer.

Act I Scene iv

At Orsino's court I am congratulated on having become so quickly a favourite with the Duke. I should do well if he continues to like me. To this slightly patronising remark I reply that if I continue to serve him well there is no reason to believe that he will not continue his friendship, unless, of course, he does not make lasting relationships. I get a very firm statement that Orsino is not inconstant.

The Duke enters and, taking me on one side, explains that since he has confided in me so freely about his love for Olivia, he has the idea that I will be an acceptable messenger. I am more likely to gain access to her than someone older and more staid. He overrides my protest. The fact that I am young and immature will give a far greater semblance of sincerity to what I am saying, and I can be more clamourous and insistent on gaining entry than someone older and more formal in manner. I agree to do my best, but, after he has gone, reveal to the audience that I am in love with him myself.

Information gained: I make a convincing boy, even if I do look rather girlish. I am in love with Orsino. I have to go on an errand to Olivia and I am not in a position to refuse. Just how I feel about it I shall find out in the course of the rehearsal.

Act I Scene v

I appear at Olivia's court. It would seem that I have carried out to the letter my instruction to be clamourous and not take no for an answer. I have done it well enough to have defeated Malvolio, who has had to retreat for further instruction. I am shown in.

At this point, to get the fun of the scene, there should be several women in black with their veils down. Unfortunately, few companies can afford extras. When there are enough ladies, it is a visual effect not rivalled until Jack Worthing makes his entrance in deep mourning for a non-existent brother. Otherwise, the effect is completely lost and when there are only two ladies present and dressed so that one is obviously a maid, it does not make much sense for Viola to ask which is the lady of the house.

The dialogue suggests that there are surreptitious giggles from behind the veils, especially as the lady who says that she will speak for Olivia is certainly not taking me seriously: she refuses to hear my carefully prepared speech and tells me to say what I have to say as briefly as possible. Exasperated, I refuse to tell it except to her alone. She dismisses her attendants but keeps up her bantering tone. It seems that she cannot be persuaded to take any message from Orsino. I ask to see her face. More banter, but she lifts her veil. She speaks of showing me the picture. I do not respond at once and she has to ask if it is not well done. She is obviously used to having immediate and ecstatic reactions to her beauty. My reply – 'Excellently done, if God did all' – provokes a calmly assured response that she does not use paint. Still using the image of a picture and painting, I assure her that her beauty is 'truly blent'. This gives me the opportunity to reproach her for not marrying and having children to immortalise her beauty. She still will not be serious, and jokes about making a will in which her good points will be itemised. She ends by asking if I was sent to 'praise' her – possibly in the sense of 'appraise' or value her. This provokes me into telling her that she overvalues herself, that Orsino's love could be no more than recompensed, even if her beauty were considered to be without equal.

Serious for the first time, Olivia asks how Orsino loves her. I do my best to tell her – 'with adorations, fertile tears, with groans that thunder love, with sighs of fire' – and get in return a simple statement of her problems. She sees that Orsino is the kind of man that any woman would want and she is generous in her praise of him, but she cannot love him and has told him so long since. I tell her that were I in Orsino's place I would not give up, and go on to tell her what I would do, which is certainly as extravagant as any lover could be expected to do.

This does not quite have the intended effect. The lady seems to be showing an interest in me. She tells me to say to Orsino that she cannot love him, and suggests that I should come back to tell her how he takes it! She gets very grand and tries to tip me, which annoys me so much that I tell her to keep her purse and hope that if she falls in love she will experience what it feels like to be rejected herself. I bid her farewell.

Information gained: It would seem that I am extremely good at being a boy. It probably helps having a twin brother. I know exactly how to do it. Several times in the scene it see that I am thinking like a boy. Perhaps, momentarily, I am Sebastian. I am quick-witted in a boyish way and not prepared to take too much nonsense from the lady. My 'willow cabin' speech might well be derived from how I know Sebastian would deal with the situation. My anger at the end might well come out of an envy of her. What would I not give to be in her place?

I must check over some of those quick verbal exchanges that I have with Olivia and the one I have with Maria. The first has to do with learning a part and being an actor; then, with Maria, sailing terms are used; then, an extended exchange on divinity. It would seem that these Elizabethans competed with one another to see who could get control of the situation by an elegant management of words. A little like a beautifully controlled fencing bout.

Act II Scene ii

This scene contains one of the most famous speeches in all drama. One which gets flogged to death as an audition speech by over-eager beginners and which is regarded with some trepidation by the more experienced.

On my way back to Orsino I am alone – my attendants were probably dismissed when I was given admittance to Olivia – when I am overtaken by the pompous gentleman who interviewed me at Olivia's gate. He first asks if I am the young man who was with Olivia (which he must know, since he let me in). Then he holds out a ring, saying that Olivia returns it to me and that she wants no more to do with Orsino. I am never to come again on his behalf, unless it is to report his taking of the ring. It would seem that Olivia is being indiscreet. I cannot possibly take the ring, so I must hastily pretend that I brought it and that she accepted it. To my astonishment I am told that I threw it at her and that she does not mind if it is thrown back. Whereupon the disagreeable gentleman drops the ring on the ground and departs.

I must explore this speech by going through the actions, remembering that thoughts are actions – actions of the mind. I will look at the structure of the speech carefully. It will give me the right pauses.

There is an obvious pause after the first half-line, 'I left no ring with her.' When a preposterous statement has been made, one tends to repeat it in order to see if there could be any truth in it. Then the query – what does the lady mean? – followed by a thought that may have been surfacing in my mind as I walked away from the house: I hope that she does not find me attractive. Think back and remember her behaviour. Three lines of quick recollection; the third is end-stopped after the word 'distractedly'. Pause to realise what has happened: she is in love with me. There is further evidence in her sending the messenger after me.

I realise that I am holding the ring. 'None of my lord's ring! Why, he sent her none.' In some texts the first sentence has a query instead of an exclamation mark. The second sentence is the kind of reassurance that one gives oneself in a situation like this (no, I did not make a mistake – I am not going dotty!). The first sentence you can make either a query or an exclamation as you find most suitable. When in doubt about the punctuation of a line it is a good idea to get hold of another edition. Scholars may be fussy about punctuation, but the actress has to select what helps her to make the sense clear to the audience.

The realisation – 'I am the man' – can be fun, and there is the quick realisation that it is not funny for poor Olivia. Half-a-dozen lines where I consider the situation – that disguise can lead to difficulty – then a comment on women in general: they are all too easily taken in by appearance. Back to the immediate situation, exploring it, wondering how it will work out, then deciding to leave it to time – as I did in the first scene.

Information gained: I live in the present. I am adept at improvising, what we should now call 'playing it by ear'. I can see a situation as both funny and sad. 'My state is desperate for my master's love.' But I do not make an undue fuss about this. That too has an element of comedy: 'I, poor monster, fond as much on him'.

Act II Scene iv

We are back in Orsino's court. As usual, the Duke wants music, a particular song, one that suits his present mood. He is told that the singer is not here. It is Feste the jester who should sing it. He must be sent for and the musicians in the meantime must play the tune.

Why does Viola not sing it? She has told us that she can sing. Most scholars give the explanation that at the first performance the boy player was at the age when his voice was beginning to change. He could speak Viola's lines but could not be trusted with the song. However, nothing is lost by this pause, because Shakespeare takes time to explore the relationship between Viola and Orsino, who again (and it would seem as usual) wants to talk about himself as the great lover.

He breaks off to ask me how I like the music. I reply in a way that suggests that I have heard the music as an appropriate comment on his words. He is surprised at my perception, and now, showing a sensitive interest in someone else, wants to know if I am in love. My reply is simple but evasive. Orsino pressures me. He wants to know what the woman I love is like. In appearance, not unlike him, I reply. He responds (with unexpected modesty) that she cannot be worthy of me and wants to know her age. His age, I say. This provokes him to insist that the man should be the elder, so that the woman may adapt to him. (It would seem that he is older than Olivia!) He goes on to contradict what he said earlier by admitting that men are more fickle than women – which suggests that he is beginning to doubt his own sincerity. I agree with him about women. I am probably playing the boy who is trying to be as sophisticated as the older man. Encouraged by my agreement, Orsino concludes his advice about loving a woman older than myself: a woman's beauty does not last. Again I agree.

The conversation is interrupted by the arrival of Feste who sings the lovely 'Come Away, Death'. In the exchange between the Duke and Feste which follows, and the jester's references to 'opal' and 'changeable taffeta', there is a strong suggestion that Feste has his own shrewd opinion of Orsino's character. Almost as though in defiance of Feste's remarks, the Duke orders me to go again to Olivia, once again proclaiming the nobleness of his passion. I point out that the lady has said she cannot love him.

Male vanity will not take no for an answer. I tell him, this time with no tactful boyish agreement, but with straightforward honesty, that he must accept her decree. Then, trying reason, I use the example of a woman hopelessly in love with him. But my example is dismissed. Having said earlier that women are more loving and loyal than men, he now contradicts himself, forcefully rebuking me for daring to compare any woman's love with what he feels for Olivia. This is too much and I come out with, 'Ay, but I know.' It is a short line, allowing Orsino time to feel surprise before he asks what I know. In the simplest possible way I tell him what a woman can feel. I describe my own feelings, attributing them to an imaginary sister, then I echo Feste – in matters of love men profess more than they feel.

Orsino, somewhat awed by my sister's sad story, inquires if she died. I reply that I am my father's only daughter, then add, 'And all the brothers too'. Then I remember my hope that Sebastian may not be drowned. Wanting to change the subject, I quickly suggest that I go again to Olivia.

Information gained: The changes of mood from the boy to the girl are more marked here. In the early part of the scene I am the page, the perfect courtier, agreeing and sympathising with Orsino. After the song and Feste's comments my feelings as a woman are uppermost. I do not want to go to Olivia again. After the episode of the ring it would be embarrassing, and anyway, she stated very clearly that she could not love him. I use my own situation: I do not have to invent any imaginary circumstances to make him see reason. However, he is off again declaring that no woman can love as he does, which provokes my involuntary outburst that I know they can!

The scene is one of extraordinary tension and delicacy. There is a strong contrast of character. I, Viola, love Orsino but see him for what he is. I can see that his love for Olivia is largely an illusion, but that, having worked himself up and presented himself to his entire entourage as a great lover, it is difficult for him to back down. When he asks if Cesario's sister died of her love, is he thinking that something similar might be expected of him? The scene is full of marvellous possibilities. Do not make decisions too soon. Explore them all in rehearsal. Do not be afraid to play the ambiguity. An audience loves to feel that they know more about a situation than the characters themselves.

Act III Scene i

I am back at Olivia's. I meet Feste on the way. Is my relationship with him a touch spiky? Well, I am doing what Maria did earlier – and what Feste patently does not like. Professional fools were expected to get the laughs, and it seems to have been the custom that those whom he met should play the straight man in the act, so as not to enter into any sort of competition. Maria dared to be witty on her own account and so now does this strange young man of the Duke's. Feste makes it plain that he does not care for this behaviour and even hints that he knows quite a lot about 'Cesario' and his relationship with the Duke. Somewhat condescendingly, after being well tipped, he tells me that he will announce my arrival. Left alone, I reflect on the work of the professional jester, recognising that to do his job well he must be no fool.

Sir Toby and Sir Andrew appear and make the mistake of thinking that I am a stupid nonentity. Verbally, I give as good as I get. Olivia enters and I greet her in the elaborate formal manner which was then fashionable, and which I tried to use in my first meeting with her. Andrew, listening, memorises what I have said for use in a further encounter with Olivia. Olivia orders them both away, making it clear that she wishes to be alone with me.

She asks my name. I tell her, using the formality of the third person to explain that I am Cesario and that I am her servant. (At this period and for many years after, to say 'your servant' to someone was merely showing polite respect.) Olivia takes me up on this. I am servant to Orsino. The Duke is her servant, so I must be her servant's servant. It is a tricky situation because the word has several meanings. It could mean someone who did menial tasks; it could mean someone employed around the court as Cesario is; or it could be used in a romantic sense to suggest an admirer. So I say that I am the Duke's servant, meaning that I hold an official position and that I am here on his behalf. I am trying to keep it formal but she will not take the hint, telling me that she has no interest in Orsino but is more than willing to listen to a declaration from me. I attempt to stop her, but she goes on pouring out her feeling. When she asks me to tell her how I feel, I can only say that I pity her. She snatches at that to say that pity is a degree to love. Becoming more desperate, I tell her no, that often we pity enemies.

At this the lady pulls herself together, remembers her dignity, and quite graciously dismisses me. With relief I start to go, merely reminding her that Orsino is still available. I almost succeed in getting my own way when she stops me and asks the really embarrassing question – what do I think of her? My wit comes to my rescue: 'That you do think you are not what you are.' In other words: 'You do not think you are in love with a woman, but you are!' Of course Olivia misunderstands this. She thinks that Cesario is reminding her she has forgotten her rank in making overtures to a servant. She, perhaps harking back to the moment of 'five-fold blazon', indicates that my rank may be higher than I pretend. Perhaps a little weary by now, I tell her I am not what I am. Olivia persists. The irony of the situation is no longer amusing but I can only deal with it by playing on words. She is making a fool of me by her persistence, but I am making a fool of her by deceiving her. This provokes an extended outburst to which I respond firmly and truthfully that I can never love a woman and that I am not bringing any more messages from Orsino.

Information gained: I am a sympathetic person. I try to save Olivia. I might have been jealous and taken out my own frustration on her, but instead I see her as someone in the same position as me and I feel for her. I think she may be young and impulsive, having to play the great lady before she has quite grown up. She is used to being admired. She cannot quite believe it when someone is not in love with her at first sight. Hence her persistence, poor girl. Orsino's idolatry has not been good for her.

Act III Scene iv
Olivia having sent after me, I can do no more in courtesy than return. It is just possible she has changed her mind about Orsino. She has not, but I stick firmly to his message and refuse to discuss her feelings. I am dismissed, but with a final comment on her passion for me: 'A fiend like thee might bear my soul to hell.'

She leaves before I can reply, and Sir Toby and Sir Andrew appear again. It appears that Sir Andrew has taken offence and wants to fight me! I try to get this chap Fabian, who seems to have some sense, to explain what I am supposed to have done and intercede for me, but all the advice I get is that Andrew is a fine swordsman and 'Give ground if you see him furious'. There seems to be no way out, but I have no sooner drawn my sword than a strange man enters and comes between us, offering me his protection. Sir Andrew backs away at once, but Sir Toby confronts the stranger.

While they are squaring up I find myself close to Sir Andrew and ask him quietly to put up his sword. Equally quietly, he agrees. Sir Toby and the stranger have hardly begun their fight when the Duke's officers arrive and arrest my rescuer, who turns to me and says that he was searching for me. Small wonder that I look amazed. Before I have time to question him, he asks me to return some of the money that he lent me. I have no idea what he is talking about but since he has shown me 'fair kindness', I offer to give him half of what I have in my purse. This provokes an angry tirade and he accuses me of ingratitude. I reply with some spirit that ingratitude is a quality that I detest but that I do not know him, nor any other kindness he has done me. The stranger resists being dragged away by the officers and tells all present that he rescued me from the jaws of death and has cared for me ever since! And now I deny him! He is taken away, full of righteous indignation, but he has spoken the name Sebastian, which prompts me to speak some of my most wonderful lines –

Prove true, imagination, O prove true,
That I, dear brother, be now ta'en for you!

– and leave, full of hope for my brother's survival.

Information gained: I have gained in confidence, since I manage to deal with Olivia firmly but tactfully, maintaining the fact that I am Orsino's messenger. I deal quite well with Sir Toby on verbal terms, but I do not know how to talk myself out of fighting a duel. I take advantage of the fact that a stranger has come to my rescue to do a deal with Sir Andrew, who, I realise, is as scared as I am. I am amazed by the stranger's accusations, but take fresh hope at his mention of Sebastian. After he has gone I am ecstatic. In this one scene, I demonstrate control of my feelings in the public arena, but once alone, tremendous release.

Act V Scene i

Here I arrive with Orsino. He has, it seems, at last decided to visit Olivia himself. He is waylaid by Feste, who behaves with him as he did with me, but the Duke, unlike me, graciously plays the straight man and is generous in his reward. He knows the going rate!

The officers arrive with the stranger and I learn his name – Antonio – whom the officers say is a well-known pirate. I am quick to explain to the Duke that this is the man who rescued me (clearly, I must have already told him about the incident) but am ignored by both the Duke and Antonio. Olivia appears, more or less ignores the Duke in spite of his fulsome greeting and insists on addressing me as though we had some very intimate relationship. This I find alarming, as Orsino becomes jealous to the point of threatening violence, first against Olivia and then against me.

I am now forced to declare my love for Orsino – although I still do not reveal that I am a girl – and am about to leave with Orsino when Olivia calls me 'husband'. I deny it, but the Duke is furious. I have just time for one desperate protest before Sir Andrew arrives with his head bandaged and accuses me of wounding him. I deny hurting him and remind him that we have made a pact, but he persists in this accusation. Sir Toby enters with a further story of having been wounded by me. Before I can make any attempt to clear myself, a marvellous thing happens – Sebastian appears!

He does not see me at first and apologises to Olivia for having hurt her kinsman, Sir Andrew, explaining that he did not begin the attack. Olivia stares at him with astonishment. The Duke exclaims in amazement. Sebastian greets Antonio, and following the man's confused gaze – 'Which is Sebastian?' – finally turns to me. He sees me first as a mirror image. Then, gradually realising that I might be his sister, demands to know who I am. Not yet quite believing, I tell him, voicing my fear that he may be a ghost 'come to fright us', but Sebastian quickly dispels that fear: he is a spirit, but a live one. We exchange quick, confirming details about our father, and go on to tell each other what has happened. Sebastian explains the facts to the astonished Olivia: 'You are betrothed both to a maid and man.' Orsino quickly assures her she has not married beneath her and turns to me to ask if I meant what I said about loving him? I assure him I meant every word. He takes me by the hand and wants to see me in my own clothes. I tell him, in my last speech in the play, that the captain who brought me safely ashore is now in prison following an accusation by Malvolio.

I have no more share in the action of the play, but watch as Olivia and Orsino firmly sort out the remaining complications. I am given no lines of acceptance of Orsino's decision to marry me, but since I have been declaring my love for him all through the play, and in very beautiful language, the audience must know by now that I would have no objection!

Information gained from the play as a whole

How much extra understanding have I got from this careful study? Does it differ from my first impression?

I should now consider the physicality of the character. I must be convincing as a boy, or the other characters will appear stupid to be taken in by my disguise. Of course, much will depend on the kind of costume I am given. The doublet and hose worn by the Elizabethan gentleman, with its elaborate padding and shaped waist would have been a complete disguise for any girl, and the boy player wearing such a costume could easily have suggested that there was a girl inside it. If I am playing the part in a workshop situation then probably jeans and a long jacket would give the right suggestion. But I must think about my walk – a longer stride than usual: not difficult for Viola and probably enjoyable because she is free of petticoats. Two important questions to consider are: when are the moments that I need to impress other people with my masculinity, and when are the moments that I can relax and just for a moment forget that I am meant to be a man?

I must study my lines. I think this is a better phrase than 'learn my lines'. One learns a lesson, but one studies a part, going over it carefully and being sure of one's accuracy. If the words are not right, then the thought is not right; if the thought is not right, then the feeling is not right. If you are 'slow of study' like Snug in *A Midsummer Night's Dream*, it is better to learn a short section very thoroughly and prepare your reading carefully so that you can relate to the other actors, rather than come to rehearsal with a complete scene that is not accurate and having to take frequent prompts. As well as helping you understand the situation and your relationship to the other characters, a well-prepared reading will make it easier to memorise the next section.

If the director wants lines learnt as soon as possible (and it is very difficult to direct an actor who does not know his lines) explain your problem and tell him what, with his agreement, you propose to do. This may dismay him if he is short of rehearsal time, in which case you will have to do what actors have always done – stay up all night until you know it.

You may feel a bit tired and hesitant in rehearsal the next day but do not let that worry you. A couple of run-throughs later it will have paid off. You will be able to take direction with ease and confidence. All that has happened is that you have learned to work faster without diminishing your ability to see into the soul of the character.

You have done your homework. In the next and final blueprint, I will be looking at a much shorter part in a more modern play but you will see how important such homework is, and how much the actor must do to find the part.

books

Life doesn't change
it always goes on the same

people will fly about in balloons
the cut of their coats will be different
the sixth sense will be discovered
and possibly even developed and used for all I know

but I believe life itself
will remain the same

still difficult
and full of mystery
and full of happiness

Lieutenant Nikolai Lvovich Toozenbach

1 Acting

There are many books about acting. You may find that your tutors will advise against reading books about acting. The reason is that most are describing problems of acting that only professional actors have experienced and understand.

Even Stanislavski never worked with absolute beginners but with young immature actors whom he had carefully auditioned to make sure that they would understand what he was talking about. In *An Actor Prepares* **(Penguin)** he pretends that the students Tortsov is teaching are beginners, but the mistakes they make are of course the mistakes that lead Tortsov to give the right lesson: they enable him to reprove the students for showing off and trying to attract the attention of the audience – a fault which was prevalent among many professional actors at the time Stanislavski began to direct.

I have found that real beginners are usually too frightened even to look at one another, let alone the audience. But it suited Stanislavski to pretend that Tortsov's students were all beginners. Otherwise those young actors who had worked in the series of 'studios' Stanislavski created with such passionate enthusiasm might have been hurt and have felt themselves mocked if there was any suggestion that some of those students that Tortsov taught could really have known better.

There are some splendid books about Stanislavski which are probably better read after you have been at drama school a year. There is a biography of Soviet actor and director Evgeny Vakhtangov, who joined the Moscow Art Theatre under Stanislavski. He was Stanislavski's favourite pupil and went on to become a great theatrical innovator. The quotation at the very end of this book is by Vakhtangov – a beautifully evocative description of the mysterious process of acting.

In Vakhtangov's biography there is the best photograph of Stanislavski I have ever encountered: it tells you more about the man than any other I have seen. He is looking past the camera. His hand is over his mouth and he is laughing. Someone has obviously made a monumental boob but he doesn't want to hurt their feelings. His dark eyes are full of laughter and kindness.

This photo should really be the frontispiece to *My Life in Art* **(Penguin)** – a book Stanislavski was reluctant to write as he disliked the usual star biography, which he felt to be nothing but a boring relation of one success after another. I have already mentioned this and two of his other books (TECHNIQUE: A FEW DEFINITIONS) when I touched on Stanislavski and method acting. *My Life in Art* is quite a good book to read once you know something about the theatre. Then you will be able to appreciate what he has to say about Chekhov and Gorky and enjoy both his passionate enthusiasm for the theatre and his own absurd behaviour when very young – of which he frequently makes fun.

Stanislavski's enthusiasm is infectious but the conditions in which he was able to work in pre-revolutionary Russia makes him seem at times very remote from us. Again and again he talks of the experimental work that he did, but what astonishes, reading him today, is the huge amounts of money that were always available. Stanislavski was a wealthy man, and he was but one of a group of immensely wealthy men in Moscow who were interested in the Arts, who supported opera and ballet as well as theatre and bought extensively from the greatest painters of the day. One of these wealthy men financed the Moscow Art Theatre in its early days. It would seem there was never any need to economise on settings, special music, costumes, or rehearsal time (no Equity regulations). If a show was not ready, the presentation was held back until it was!

Should you hear talk about the method and method acting and want to discover more, the best book to make you understand what the talk is all about is *Method or Madness* **by Robert Lewis (Samuel French Inc)**. Himself a member of the famous Group theatre with Elia Kazan and Cheryl Crawford, he started the Actors' Studio. In 1957 he gave a series of nine lectures in the Playhouse, New York. These lectures became famous and may still be read in this book. At once profound and very funny, Robert Lewis understands Stanislavski and is splendid at pointing out how the teaching of the 'master' has so frequently been misrepresented by so-called disciples. The book also makes one realise very clearly the difference between the way an American actor gets his training and the ways of study open to European actors.

Whilst reading about Stanislavski you should also read:

The Letters of Anton Chekhov **(Various editions are available)** These letters recount Chekhov's experiences in the theatre both before and after his meeting with Stanislavski and give descriptions of theatre procedure at that time, as well as an overall account of life in Russia.

The Lower Depths **and other plays by Maxim Gorky (Yale University)** Gorky wrote of the Russia of his day from 'the lower depths' through various grades of life – as he experienced it – in the period prior to the Revolution. He will give you an idea of how the other half lived.

Finally, in my section VOICE I mention a splendid book which is not now in print and may not be easy to get hold of: *The Irresistible Theatre* **by W Bridge Adams (Secker & Warburg).** But if you do come across it in a second-hand bookshop or library, it is well worth reading.

2 Shakespeare

For the understanding of Shakespeare get a good edition of the complete works. The Alexander text – *The Complete Works of William Shakespeare* **edited by Peter Alexander (Collins)** – is now in paperback. It has good print, an excellent introduction, explanatory notes on the text and a useful glossary. It is the text the BBC used for the complete series of Shakespeare's plays televised in the late Seventies and early Eighties (now available on video). Avoid editions with very small print and 'quaint' Victorian illustrations, and those huge 'de luxe' editions which weigh half a ton and are a real handicap in classwork. Whichever edition you decide on, remember that line numbering is essential.

Introducing Shakespeare **by G B Harrison (Penguin)** is a must. The best possible start for your library. A pocket-book but wonderfully comprehensive. Lovely illustrations. Good book list at the back.

Shakespeare and Burbage **by Martin Holmes (Philmore and Co)**. For getting to know Shakespeare as a man of the theatre, this is a splendid book. So is *The Guns of Elsinore* by the same author. They may be out of print but will be obtainable from the library or perhaps – like many of these books about theatre and acting – from the Samuel French bookshop, 52 Fitzroy Street, London W1P 6JR, telephone 0171 387 9373.

The Living World of Shakespeare **by John Wain (Macmillan)** contains excellent down-to-earth essays on the plays.

Other books on Shakespeare that are worth studying when you are ready:

Discovering Shakespeare **by John Russell Brown (Macmillan)**. A very good book written by a scholar who, while exploring the text, believes that to be truly appreciated Shakespeare must be acted.

Playing Shakespeare **by John Barton (Methuen in association with C4 TV)**. A record of workshops made by the Royal Shakespeare Company for Channel Four. Fascinating. But since those taking part are highly experienced professionals one feels the need to hear it!

And a reminder of what I said in my section on BREATHING that if you want to know what Shakespeare was like as a person, read *Memories for Tomorrow* **by Jean-Louis Barrault (Thames & Hudson)** – especially his amazing description of the breathing process.

3 History and grammar

The two great books on the history of the theatre are *World Drama* and *The Development of the Theatre*, both by **Allardyce Nicoll (Harrap)**. Wonderful books through which one can browse for hours.

Other books on general English history are:

A Concise History of England **by F E Halliday (Thames and Hudson)**. For those of you who have not learnt English history chronologically and therefore find history plays difficult, this is a thoroughly enjoyable book. Gets it all in order and makes everything clear.

English Social History **by G M Trevelyan (Longman)**. General information about social history.

Essays in English History **by A J P Taylor (Penguin/Pelican Books)**. A study of special people in special periods by a masterly historian.

The Reason Why **by Cecil Woodham-Smith (Constable)**
A book of real insight and marvellous ironic writing about the Victorian period.

The Lisle Letters **edited by Muriel St Clare Byrne (Penguin)** and anything else you can get hold of by this author, including: *Elizabethan Life in Town and Country*. She is enthusiastic, witty and deeply understanding of human nature. She can make you believe you lived in the period.

Now for the book promised in my section on grammar in SPEECH:

Longman English Grammar **by L G Alexander (Longman)**. This is for those of you who did not learn English grammar at school. Excellent, comprehensive, arranged in such a way that you have immediate access to the information you need.

4 General reading

Novels, novels and yet again novels. Jane Austen, Dickens, the Brontës, George Eliot, Thackeray and Trollope. These are just the English writers. Their books are full of information about the manners and customs and the social values of the period in which they wrote. Such novels are far more valuable than any specialist books on manners and customs because these authors are writing about how their characters are affected by those values. Some of you may have read Louisa May Alcott's *Little Women* and the problems Jo and Meg had when going to stay with rich friends. Today our dress is superficially simpler, but the snobbishness of fashion remains. Two handbags may be almost identical but one bears the Gucci label. Even jeans are more important when they have a designer label. (See PRACTICALITIES: COMEDY AND STYLE)

Toozenbach, the lieutenant in Chekhov's *Three Sisters*, says life does not change: 'People will fly about in balloons, the cut of their coats will be different, the sixth sense will be discovered, and possibly even developed and used, for all I know… But I believe that life itself will remain the same; it will still be difficult and full of mystery and full of happiness.'

It is a speech to keep in mind no matter what character one is playing.

blueprint interesting problems

Soliony *Three Sisters*

Most drama schools give students an opportunity to experience working with Chekhov – if not in a full-scale production then in a workshop, usually during the first year. Like Shakespeare, Chekhov draws his characters in depth and the actor learns to look deeply into the text to discover what he must reveal. Once students become used to a different idiom of speech they have great enjoyment in working on the plays. I have chosen here to go through the character of Vassily Vassilich Soliony from *Three Sisters* because the character presents the actor with some interesting problems.

First reading

A first reading of the play reveals that Captain Soliony is a strange person who takes pride in being strange, that he believes himself to resemble Lermontov, that he has a habit of spraying himself with scent, that he is in love with Irena and that he has fought two duels. In the fourth act he kills Lieutenant Toozenbach.

No one seems to like him except Toozenbach, who likes everyone, but Soliony nonetheless seems to come and go in the Prozorov household much as he pleases. Two things to remember here: Russians are hospitable (hospitality seems to be part of their nature) and the Prozorovs have since their father's time kept open house for the officers of his regiment. It is not quite as it was in his day. His was probably a charismatic personality and while he was alive there was money to spend on entertaining. Olga, the schoolmistress, and Andrey, the shy, violin-playing university student, are not likely to attract soldiers in search of entertainment. But Soliony has one overriding reason for being there – Irena.

That is information from your first read-through, but it would seem that research on the part of the actor is necessary even if the director has talked about the background of the play and its meaning. The actor playing Soliony may feel he needs more detail than the director has time to give. There are some books which can help: *Letters of Anton Chekhov* (see BOOKS ABOUT ACTING); *Lermontov* by Janko Lavrin (Bowes and Bowes, Cambridge); *Hero of Our Time* by Mikhail Yurevich Lermontov himself (this Penguin paperback edition has been in print since the BBC broadcast a dramatised version and has a useful introduction about Lermontov), and lastly *The Penguin Book of Russian Verse* (edited by J M Cohen) – the poems are in Russian but there are English prose translations with each one. You will find here the poem by Pushkin which Masha quotes in Act I and several by Lermontov, which will give you something of his quality as a poet – though Soliony seems more interested in the proud, arrogant side of his personality.

Act I

In the first act Soliony seems to do nothing but make awkward remarks and annoy people. The actor has a problem in the first act. How is he to suggest that Soliony is obsessed with Irena? She tells Toozenbach near the end of the act that she dislikes Soliony. She cannot say that unless she has a reason for it. If Soliony has done nothing more dangerous than behave like a social misfit, there is no reason for her remark. But what if he spends all the time looking at her, so that she keeps seeing his concentrated gaze across the room? If she thought him attractive this would please her, but because she does not, and because he is a powerful personality – something dark and strange, possibly dangerous – he frightens her.

Soliony has only about a dozen lines in Act I and each seems to be intended to make someone else uncomfortable and show himself off as someone witty and attractive. None of these efforts is successful. All he does is irritate people. So why does he do it?

We know that Soliony believes himself to resemble Lermontov, the poet and novelist whose reputation was second only to Pushkin. A romantic and charismatic figure, Lermontov was banished to the Caucasus and wrote the semi-autobiographical novel *Hero of Our Time* shortly before his death in a duel in 1841. It is recorded that he could be sitting silent in a corner of a room in which a group of people were conversing. Suddenly he would make a remark and from then on all the conversation, all the attention, centred around him. Soliony, like many shy people, is desperate for attention and secretly sees himself as a romantic hero like Lermontov. He does what shy people so often do: he makes remarks which, though not unintelligent, are wrongly timed and not appropriate to the subject under discussion.

Act II

A social situation, and Soliony manages for once to make himself quite popular by making a ridiculous, rather rudely teasing remark to Natasha who has been boring everybody about her baby Bobik.

The samovar has just been brought, which is a sign for Russians to gather round and talk. Soliony enters, bows to the company and sits at the table. Of course those around the table should bow an acknowledgment. Natasha is dominating the conversation with her everlasting talk of her baby. Soliony has his one big social moment in his line about Bobik – 'If that child were mine, I'd cook him up in a frying pan and eat him' – and picking up his glass of tea, he retreats to a corner. He has had the sense to make a good exit. Toozenbach arrives with a bottle of brandy. (In the previous act he has said that Soliony is alright when you get him alone.) Soliony begins to talk of himself. He explains that he is awkward in company. He then goes on to liken himself to Lermontov, even to say that he has been told he looks like Lermontov. He takes out his scent bottle and sprinkles some on his hands.

Here it is important to remember that in the early nineteenth century the great romantic role model was Lord Byron. Both Pushkin and Lermontov had been influenced by his poetry. Lermontov was also influenced by Byron's personality. Byron died in Greece while helping the Greeks to fight for their freedom. Lermontov died in a duel over a personal matter. Is Soliony thinking of this when he uses the scent?

It would seem that Toozenbach finds Soliony's idea of his resemblance to Lermontov embarrassing. He turns the conversation to the fact that he has resigned his commission, explaining that he is going to work. Then as Chebutykin ambles up, telling Irena about life in the Caucasus, Soliony turns on him. Is there a flash of jealousy because there is a close relationship between Chebutykin and Irena? Is this what provokes Soliony to endeavour to put Chebutykin down over something so simple as the difference between chehartma and cheremsha.

The potential row is calmed by Andrey and Toozenbach but it begins again with the mention of Moscow University. Toozenbach's friendly, slightly drunken proposal that he should accompany Andrey to Moscow provokes Soliony to insist on his superior knowledge by declaring that there are two universities in Moscow. His lack of sensitivity does not let him recognise that everyone else is in party mood and therefore does not care how many universities there are in Moscow.

Soliony takes himself off to another room. This seems a little strange. When there is a disagreement among guests, usually one or other will leave the house. But Soliony behaves like one of a very large family in a large house. There is room for him to take his bad humour somewhere else.

When he re-enters it is to find Irena alone. Realising that the carnival party has gone, he makes the slightly ominous remark, 'Then you're alone here?' At this period, for a young girl to be alone with a man, particularly late at night, could be seen as compromising. For such a situation to occur it meant that either the man was about to offer marriage – or something less proper. A girl finding herself in such a situation was expected to give the man a signal that his attentions were not wanted. To allow him to make any kind of proposition and then turn him down was thought inconsiderate and unladylike. So after a slight pause to give him an opportunity to say goodnight himself, Irena says it.

But Soliony does not acknowledge the signal. He plunges into exactly the kind of declaration Irena does not wish to hear. She gives him the opportunity to behave correctly by again asking him to go and bidding him goodnight. But he is much more concerned with his passion for her than with her feelings and presses on, using high-flown language. Again she tries to stop him. Again he goes on.

Then in the middle of his speech comes a strange stage direction – 'Rubs his forehead' – after which he ceases to pressure her and recognises that he cannot force her to love him. Something has to happen here to make him change. It can only be some strong gesture of rejection from Irena. This is something that actors and director must work out between them. He probably makes some kind of physical contact from which she pulls away with instinctive dislike: she finds him physically repellent and he realises it. His anger at this provokes his threat against any possible rivals. But Chekhov brilliantly prevents the scene from becoming melodramatic by bringing in Natasha and giving Soliony a wonderful exit.

Act III

Here Soliony has only one entrance and two speeches.

He walks into Irena's bedroom which she is now sharing with Olga and which, since the usurpation of her own room by Natasha, seems to have become a family sitting-room. When he comes in, Irena, not surprisingly, asks him to leave. His first response is to demand why the Baron can come in and he can't. Vershinin covers the situation by saying they must all go and tries to divert attention by asking what is happening at the fire.

Soliony is not to be diverted. He replies casually to Vershinin and returns to the attack. He is obviously jealous of Toozenbach. There is a moment between Masha and Vershinin and then the latter suggests that he and Soliony go to the ballroom. As Vershinin is his superior officer, Soliony cannot refuse. He goes out after having quoted once again from Krylov, this time from his poem 'The Geese' (which you will find in *The Penguin Book of Russian Verse* – you can discover for yourself why Soliony quotes it here).

Act IV

The stage direction tells us that Soliony enters at the back of the stage with two officers who merely cross the stage. They are going to officiate at the duel. Soliony comes down to Chebutykin to summon him as the doctor who must be present. He greets Andrey, casually assuming that he does not know what is happening. When Chebutykin gathers himself together wearily, Soliony mocks him as he had mocked Masha in the first act. Chebutykin grumbles at him and Soliony says he has no intention of killing Toozenbach, he'll merely wound him. He takes out his scent bottle and for the first time we are told why he scents his hands – they smell of death. Then he quotes those two amazing lines by Lermontov about rebelliously seeking a storm – as if there were tranquillity in storms.

Chebutykin repeats the lines from the Russian fable that Soliony quoted, and the stage direction is: 'Goes out with Soliony.' But in the original Moscow Art production something different happened. Soliony remained alone on stage looking up at Irena's window. John Fernald, in his book, *A Sense of Direction*, describes how the Russian actor Livanov considered his love for Irena and contemplated in silence that it might be he, not Toozenbach, who could be killed. The pause was long and the suspense extraordinary. Eventually, he stamped out his cigarette and quickly left the stage in the direction Soliony had gone.

ending

A man's personality takes shape over the years that make up his life. They give his face its features and determine his physiognomy. His entire spiritual structure and attitude to life are also shaped day by day.

That is why a person reacts to events exactly as he should react. He is not concerned about behaving consistently, according to the logic of his inner being. Nature takes care of this and a man's reactions take place unconsciously. The core of his personality is already formed. A man has moments when he wants to live and joyfully senses his participation in everything living. He becomes cheerful and energetic and his good and bad sides show themselves especially vividly.

At moments like these a man becomes inspired, his eyes sparkle and he is brimming with a desire to do something. This is a festive moment.

This happens to actors too.

Day by day, rehearsal by rehearsal, the actor's role in the given play takes shape.

Grain by grain, the actor unconsciously accumulates inside himself everything he needs for his role.

Then many performances take place and his work on shaping the kernel of his role continues.

The time comes when the kernel is ripe and the actor no longer has to worry about the logic of his character's inner and outer existence. The actor's own artistic nature takes care of this.

We need only this joyful sense of theatre.

We must be filled with a desire to 'reveal', in other words, to create...

Evgeny Vakhtangov
from the 'Impressions Book' of the Arts Theatre Studio 21
September 1916